Pregnant and Single

Pregnant and Single

Help for the tough choices

Carolyn Owens and Linda Roggow MSW

PYRANEE BOOKS

Zondervan Publishing House
Grand Rapids, Michigan

PREGNANT AND SINGLE
Copyright © 1984, 1990 by Linda Roggow and Carolyn Owens

Pyranee Books is an imprint of Zondervan Publishing House,
1415 Lake Drive, S.E., Grand Rapids, Michigan 49506.

Library of Congress Cataloging-in-Publication Data

Owens, Carolyn Pearl.
    Pregnant and single / Carolyn Owens and Linda Roggow.
        p.   cm.
    Rev. ed. of: Handbook for pregnant teenagers.   1984.
    Includes bibliographical references.
    ISBN 0-310-45821-8
    1. Unmarried mothers—United States. 2. Pregnancy, Unwanted—
United States. 3. Teenage mothers—United States. 4. Teenage
pregnancy—United States. I. Roggow, Linda. II. Owens, Carolyn
Pearl. Handbook for pregnant teenagers. III. Title.
HQ759.45.O94   1990
362.83'92'08352—dc20   90–8219
                                                                      CIP

Unless otherwise noted, all Scripture references are taken from the *Holy Bible: New International Version* (North American Edition), copyright © 1973, 1978, 1984 by the International Bible Society. Used by permission of Zondervan Bible Publishers.

Printed in the United States of America

90 91 92 93 94 95 96 / AF / 10 9 8 7 6 5 4 3

Dedicated to—

Our parents
  Bette and Bud Florine
  Pearl and Roland Starry
Thank you for giving us life.

Our husbands
  Paul Roggow
  Bill Owens
Thank you to the two men who
lovingly cheered us on.

Our grandmothers
  Esther Florine
  Bernice Pool
Thank you for the wonderful
influence you've had on our lives.

Our friends
  Melodee Andersen
  Melody Beattie
  Marie Gunderson
  Jeanne Spooner
  Vi Underdahl
Thank you for your editorial comments
and marvelous prayer support.

Contents

1.
Don't Panic!

Jill, twenty-one years old, has just completed her junior year at a state university. Since her sophomore year in high school, Jill has been active in church groups and is now a leader of one on her campus. But today none of those things is important.

Jill is pregnant—and unmarried.

This morning she is determined to keep an appointment, her third, at the abortion clinic. She had canceled the other two. Why? She wasn't sure. But this one she intends to keep.

She sits on the edge of her bed in the dorm room, struggling to wipe away the tears that run down her face. Jill's thoughts echo voices from the past that gossiped about another young woman in similar straits:

"Did you hear about _____ ?"

"No! Really! Tsk. Tsk. I never would have believed it."

As she caresses the cameo rose pendant Randy gave her less than three months ago, Jill catches a glimpse of a large poster on her dorm wall. It's of her and Randy looking happy, carefree, and very much in love.

Why me? Why did this happen to me?

Her thoughts begin to race: _People at home will say, "How could a nice young woman like Jill get into a mess like_ *this?" Just wait till my friends find out. They'll never understand. I'll lose their respect.*

Then she rationalizes: *I'm too young to be a parent. I want to have fun. Share good times with my friends. Go out on dates.*

Feelings of panic grip her again. Thinking about all the rumors that will spread, Jill hates the place she has put herself in: *If only I hadn't let Randy sweet-talk me, this wouldn't have happened. Love . . .* She spits the word out. It tastes bitter and slimy.

Jill knows she can't go through with this pregnancy. She'd have to leave college. How would she support herself? What about all the medical expenses? She must go through with this abortion. *After all*, she reminds herself, *it's just a problem for today. Tomorrow the baby will be gone.* Baby? Suddenly she remembers why she canceled the last two appointments. Abortion means taking a human life. She can't go through with that. She just can't.

But how can she tell her parents? They'll be hurt . . . horrified . . . ashamed. Who knows what they will think or how they will react? How can she give them this grief? How can she even face them?

But if she goes through with the abortion, how can she face God or herself? Jill looks at the phone . . .

The Cycle of Sorrow

If you're in the same situation as Jill, in the next few days, weeks, and months your emotions and physical state are going to go through some changes. Let's face it, you're never going to be the same person you were before pregnancy. You may experience quickly shifting moods. At this exact moment, your hormones are adjusting to body changes.

Just as lots of women tend to be more emotional right before their periods, you may experience those same kinds of intense feelings now. One day you may feel anxious and unsure. The next, you may be exuberant and feel more womanly, more feminine. At times, depending on your emotions and attitude, you may believe you're embarking on a new adventure. At other times, if your mood is down, you're sure you should never have been born. Any other crisis is better than the situation you are in!

In any crisis there is a seven-step "Cycle of Sorrow." The seven steps are (1) shock, (2) denial, (3) anger, (4) bargaining, (5) depression, (6) acceptance, and (7) growth. Some of these steps can overlap. We will observe this cycle through the eyes of a pregnant young woman.

1. SHOCK

Holly felt immobilized. She heard the doctor say, "You're pregnant," but she can't believe it. She doesn't "feel" pregnant.

Shock serves as a cushion, giving Holly time to absorb the fact of pregnancy. "I remember how I felt when the doctor told me," she said. "I was speechless! The shock waves were almost visible. I came home and couldn't talk or eat. All I could manage to do was stare off into space."

Shock is a defense mechanism, a buffer against the crisis. However, shock leaves as rapidly as one is able to absorb the painful reality.

2. DENIAL

Denial can last for twenty-four hours or as long as the entire pregnancy. Holly wanted to deny the circumstances; she didn't even want to think about a baby coming in nine months. Her mind fixed on the thought: This is just a temporary inconvenience.

"My denial mechanism was super strong," Holly remembered. "I was an aerobics instructor and wasn't about to give it up. But in my fourth month I saw how my body was changing and could no longer deny reality."

Sometimes a woman thinks that no one will ever find out, that the pregnancy will not affect her lifestyle. But to think she can get through this without ever telling those closest to her is unrealistic. Emotional support is especially needed at this time. Even though everything within her wants to deny the pregnancy, it's better to get the crisis out in the open.

3. ANGER

Holly's denial turned into anger: "I can't believe I got caught! It just isn't fair. Most of my friends aren't virgins. In fact, I know a lot of them really sleep around a lot. Why me?" She became angry with God, her parents, and her boyfriend, but mostly with herself.

"Talk about stupid! Why did I ever listen to Bill? Now I'm the one in trouble, and he goes on his merry way."

4. BARGAINING

At this point Holly bargained with God. "Please let this be all a big mistake," she pleaded. "If you make it disappear, I won't ever be promiscuous again." She prayed for the natural disaster of a miscarriage. But what Holly didn't realize is that bargaining is really an attempt to postpone the inevitable.

5. DEPRESSION

Depression can come at any time during a pregnancy. There is an overwhelming sense of hopelessness, despair, and a strong feeling that there is no solution. Holly became confused. She had trouble getting up for work and when she arrived at her job she couldn't concentrate.

This feeling of futility can become so extreme that a person no longer thinks rationally. Some young women become so depressed that they attempt suicide.

6. ACCEPTANCE

"In the middle of my fourth month I came to the conclusion I had better get some help," Holly said. "I'd worked through the denial, anger, bargaining, and depression and realized it was time to face my pregnancy and accept it. No matter how hard I prayed, I knew it wasn't going to go away. There wasn't going to be any miscarriage."

At this point Holly told a close friend. After many tears, and a lot of honest dialogue, her friend encouraged her to seek counseling.

7. GROWTH

"I believe these last few months have been some of the hardest I'll ever have to go through," Holly related.

"But having worked through the previous six stages, I'm now heading toward a positive resolution. For the first time, with my counselor's help and my friend's support, I can see a glimmer of light at the end of the tunnel."

It's Okay To Have Feelings!

You may be hurting right now. You may feel like kicking someone or doing something worse. It may feel like the end of the world. Your future may seem bleak and hopeless. Give yourself permission to hurt and be angry. It's okay to feel this way; but it's also important to learn how to cope with your stress in one of the most delicate times of your life.

Ways People Cope

Did you know that *your* delicate time can produce a season for potential growth by teaching you how to cope effectively? According to Gerald Caplan, leading advocate of crisis theory, the new pattern of coping that you work out to deal with this crisis can become an important way to solve all future problems. There are healthy and unhealthy ways to cope.

UNHEALTHY WAYS

A person can—

- Deny that a problem exists. (I'll wear a tight, binding girdle.)
- Refuse to seek or accept help. (I'll handle it myself.)

- Run away from it. (I'll get high to escape and forget.)
- Fail to explore alternatives. (I've made up my mind already.)
- Blame others. (It's all *his* fault.)
- Turn away from friends and family. (Everyone just leave me alone!)

HEALTHY WAYS

A person will—

- Face the problem.
- Gain a better perspective of it.
- Work through bad feelings.
- Accept responsibility for coping with the problem.
- Explore alternative ways to handle crisis.
- Distinguish between what can and cannot be changed.
- Be open to communication with people ready to support her.
- Take steps, however small, to handle the crisis positively.[1]

HOW CAN YOU COPE?

Most likely your first reaction to being pregnant was, "Help! Someone get me out of this mess!" You may think that you are at a dead end with no way out. However, this moment—the peak of your crisis—is the *worst* possible time to make any final decisions.

Today you are under much stress and pressure. Your

[1] Howard J. Clinebell, Jr., *Basic Types of Pastoral Counseling*, rev. ed. (Nashville: Abingdon Press, 1966).

coping abilities may be weak right now. Move slowly toward any solution. "Take one day at a time" is a bit of wisdom you will want to practice continually.

Positive Actions to Help You Cope

Here are some things you can do to combat your negative emotions. Participating in one or all of these will help you not only calm your thoughts, but also help you to see your situation more clearly.

- Practice relaxation exercises.
- Take hot baths.
- Sit back and take deep breaths.
- Go for long walks.
- Pray.

. . . Jill takes a deep breath and calls the abortion clinic to cancel her appointment. Then she dials again, this time a number she had copied from a poster on her apartment bulletin board.

A woman answers, "Crisis Pregnancy Center."

Pregnant and single, Jill is not alone. Lots of her counterparts are in crisis pregnancies, too. Unfortunately the fact is that in the United States alone more than one million unwed young women as well as older women, become pregnant each year—and the number is increasing rapidly.

2.
What's Happening to Me?

You are probably aware that many physical changes occur throughout pregnancy, but for those of us who need more specific information, this chapter is for you.

Something's Missing

In many but not all cases, the first change you have noticed is that your monthly flow has stopped. If you have participated in sexual intercourse, a missed menstrual period with previously regular cycles suggests pregnancy as the most likely cause.

"Filling Out"

Another physical change will be enlarged breasts due to lactation. Liquid forms inside which will increase the size of your breasts throughout pregnancy. In the beginning they will be tender, but later the sensitivity and tingling sensation will disappear. Your breasts may leak a fluid that is called colostrum. In the first few months it will look yellow and watery. However, toward the end of term the colostrum takes on an opaque, whitish appearance and resembles milk.

Upset Stomach

You may experience "morning sickness." This nausea, sometimes accompanied by vomiting, can occur at any time of the day. Although the cause is not known, some doctors think that it is a result of the hormonal changes occuring at the beginning of pregnancy. Usually "morning sickness" disappears at the end of the first trimester. During this time, you may find some foods you have always enjoyed, and even some smells, will cause nausea. Eating soda crackers and dividing your food into several small meals a day is a good idea. One caution: A pregnant woman is advised *never* to take any medicine for morning sickness without her doctor's advice.

Tired All The Time

Some women undergo great fatigue. At first you may feel as though you cannot force yourself out of bed. You may be tired all day and yearn for long afternoon naps. Generally this excessive need for sleep disappears after the first few months.

Bathroom Visits

Many women feel a frequent need to urinate. This is caused by pressure on the bladder from the growing baby. The condition usually goes away after the tenth or twelfth week, but often recurs a few weeks before delivery.

Round and Firm, But Not Flat

As your baby continues to grow, you will see a gradual enlargement of the abdomen. This is first noticeable around the twelfth week, and you will begin to "show" sometime between the sixteenth and twentieth weeks.

Streaks may form on either or both sides of your abdomen. These stretch marks, which will assume a pearl-white appearance, will get pale after pregnancy, but they will never totally disappear.

All these changes are definite signs that a baby is in the making. At this stage you may not be too concerned whether your baby has brown or blue eyes, red, black, or blond hair. Nevertheless, with each day that passes your child is being intricately formed. His eyes, facial features, arms, and legs are developing in your womb.

To help in this development, you will want to do everything necessary to ensure that the two of you come through this pregnancy in the best possible condition. Some suggestions on how to accomplish this are given in the next chapter.

3.
Healthy Mother and Baby

Society in general and medical experts in particular are learning more and more about how an unborn child is affected by its mother's health care. As you begin to feel and see the signs of pregnancy, it's important to seek good medical attention. We urgently advise you to *see a doctor*.

See a Doctor

"Numerous studies show that mothers who have early, regular prenatal care are more likely to have healthy babies than women who have little or no care. Prematurity or low-birthweight occurs two to three times more often among women who have had inadequate care" (March of Dimes Foundation–Alert Bulletin 29). Teenage pregnancy is a high-risk situation; nearly half of young pregnant women receive no prenatal care in their first trimester.

However, you will automatically lower the risk when you put yourself under the care of a competent obstetrician. Another advantage of prenatal care is that your doctor will inform you about times and locations of childbirth classes. Among other things, the classes can teach you relaxation exercises. Your visits to an obstetrician will be your education in what and what not to do during pregnancy.

"The birth of a child, a new life: everywhere in the world this is regarded as one of the most profound and important events that can happen . . . A young woman can increase her chances of producing a healthy, normal baby by knowing exactly what things can threaten her baby's development and then by avoiding them. In this way, she is already protecting and nurturing her child; in this way, she is already a good mother." Here are some facts you will want to be aware of concerning good health during pregnancy.[1]

Nutrition During Pregnancy

You may never have thought too much about nutrition before you were pregnant, but *now* it is doubly important to eat well-balanced meals.

Pregnancy is a time of such rapid growth and development that it demands good nutrition. The pregnant woman needs to fulfill nutritional requirements for both herself and her baby. Healthy eating can prevent or lessen many of the common problems faced by mother and child. Every woman, no matter what her pre-pregnancy weight is, needs to gain enough weight to maintain both her and the baby's well-being during the pregnancy.

To ensure good health and nutrition for you and your child, eat a variety of foods from the four food groups: (1) Meat, (2) dairy products, (3) fruits and vegetables, (4) breads and cereals. It's best to go easy

[1]Janet R. Johnson and Diane Pankow, *Pre-Natal Care, Loving Before Birth* (Weymouth, Massachusetts: Life Skills Education, 1989).

on snack foods and sweets, or the pounds will appear faster than you'd like. Of course, the proper amount of weight gain will vary with each person, and your doctor will advise you what your gain should be. Whether great or small, now is *not* the time to undertake a crash diet. Nor is it the time to take unnecessary drugs.

Drugs During Pregnancy

The proper use of drugs and medicine is crucial to a healthy pregnancy. No medicine *of any kind* should be taken unless advised by your doctor.

CAFFEINE

Did you know that caffeine is a drug and has been part of the human diet for several thousand years?

"It is a natural ingredient in coffee, tea, chocolate, cocoa, and some soft drinks. It is a compound that can cross the placenta to reach the fetus and has also been detected in the milk of breast-feeding mothers" (*FDA Consumer Memo*, Publ. No. 80–1079).

ALCOHOL

How many of us are aware that alcohol is considered a drug too? Lots of people use it as a form of escape, but as a pregnant woman you should be informed that "One to three out of every 1,000 newborns, or about 5,000 babies per year, are born with fetal alcohol syndrome (FAS). A new study points out that even two or three drinks a week may trigger spontaneous abortion. Since no one knows at which point in the pregnancy alcohol does the greatest damage or what amount can be consumed safely, pregnant women should drink no alcoholic beverages." ("Drugs and Pregnancy: Often the Two Don't Mix" by Evelyn Zamula in *FDA Consumer*, June 1989, 9–10.)

CIGARETTES

"Among the warnings on the packages of cigarettes is a statement that smoking may complicate pregnancy. While no specific malformations are connected with smoking, birth weight of babies born to smokers averages a half-pound less than that of non-smokers. Low birth weight babies are forty times more likely to die in infancy than those of normal weight. It is thought that nicotine, which constricts blood vessels, may reduce placental blood flow, and thus the amounts of nutrients and oxygen to the unborn baby. Smoking may also increase the risk of miscarriage, stillbirth and death in newborns." ("Drugs and Pregnancy: Often the Two Don't Mix" by Evelyn Zamula in *FDA Consumer*, June 1989, 9–10).

You can see that there are many harmful things that can endanger you and your baby's health. The next question of whom you should tell can seem even more dangerous to you than the matter of what to eat.

4.
Whom Can I Turn to?

You Are Not Alone

Being pregnant and single affects women from all areas of society, all socioeconomic levels, and all nationalities. But everyone who finds herself pregnant and single lives her own real-life drama of mental, physical and emotional strain. Each one still faces the same choices.

If you are pregnant and unmarried, a young woman living at home or perhaps away at school, or maybe out on your own with a full-time or half-time job, right now you are probably afraid, confused, and torn by many emotions. Where do you go from here? To whom can you turn? Don't despair. Your future is changed, but not finished. With careful thought and some help, opportunities are still ahead.

Whom Should I Tell?

You are probably anxious to tell someone about your pregnancy, yet afraid. But you are going to have to tell someone soon. At this point you need to think carefully about whom you tell. For one thing, as soon as you do, you will be bombarded with opinions about your situation. People will want to tell you what to do. So you need to determine who *should* be told first and prepare yourself for his or her reaction.

PARENTS

The logical place to begin, of course, is with your parents, as difficult as that may be. For instance, you may think your parents will be violently angry, perhaps enough even to disown you. You can expect that they will be hurt at first. Because parents tend to blame themselves when things like this happen, you could hear, "Where have we gone wrong? What did we ever do to deserve this?"

Your pregnancy is a crisis in their lives as well as yours. Remember how you felt when you first found out? They will have many of those same feelings. In fact, they will go through their own Cycle of Sorrow.

Many parents will try to take over the decision-making completely. Some may even say, "You're going to have an abortion, and that's final!" They may not mean that. It may just be their initial reaction since they're so used to protecting you. No one can *force* you to have an abortion against your will. Remember, your parents are in shock as well. Give them time and space to sort through their feelings.

Do you recall a time from your earlier years when you told them something with fear and trembling? Or maybe it was something your parents discovered on their own—you dented the car, lied, or cheated on a test? Did your parents come through for you at that time? If so, then there's a good possibility, after their initial shock, that they'll do it again.

A possible way to begin the conversation is, "Mom,

Dad, I love you, but I've really let you down. I'm sorry to have to tell you this . . ."

Then again, maybe you will think it best to speak with one parent at a time, or even tell an older brother or sister first. However, if you simply cannot bear the thought of dealing with their reactions at this time, how about talking with . . .

A TRUSTED FRIEND?

Can you think of someone you feel comfortable confiding in? Perhaps someone with whom you've shared good times and bad, laughter and tears. You know him or her so well that you feel confident you won't shock this person or be criticized. This is the person to confide in.

YOUR BOYFRIEND?

What about the father of your baby? Will he stand with you, or against you? Picture his reaction. Will he act unsure? Deny everything? Want to take any responsibility at all? Or do you think he'll be pleased, proud, protective, and loving?

Whatever his reaction is, it's important for the two of you to be alone when you tell him. He also needs time to sort through his feelings; so after you've talked, meet again later when he's had a chance to think about it.

However, he is not the person to make a final decision; that's for you to do. If he insists you abort, patiently let him know his opinion is important, but that *you* are the one carrying the child. If your boyfriend still lives at home, you may want to include his parents in this discussion.

If and when the meeting takes place, that is the time to get your feelings out in the open and find out what support you have. In most cases one set of parents will take a firm stance initially. When you get together to discuss the problem, you both can gain a clearer perspective of how the two of you think and feel.

You and your boyfriend will need to discuss who's going to take care of the medical bills. What about the relationship? Will it be continued? This time together will help provide direction for both you and your boyfriend, as well as your families.

PEOPLE IN YOUR CHURCH?

If you are involved in a church, one of the scariest things is wondering what the people there will say and think. How can you face them? If possible, talk with one of the spiritual leaders. He should be able to recommend a trained professional to counsel you if the church does not have a trained counselor.

If you don't have a church family, this would be a good time to find one. Do you have a couple of young friends you feel close to? Maybe you could visit their churches with them. You may feel like withdrawing from the entire human race, but seclusion won't help. Caring and concerned people will.

Dealing With Others' Reactions

As your pregnancy progresses and more people find out, you will probably meet many reactions—from total acceptance to judgmental shock. You will have to get used to the idea that some people won't accept your pregnancy. Other people's negative feelings about your situation may sometimes be the hardest thing with which to deal. People's reactions come from their own backgrounds and values. Many of them will try to suggest what you should do. You'll need to realize that their suggestions may not be appropriate for you. So after you have considered their input, make your own decision.

Then there are your friends. Some of them may actually turn against and reject you. The truth is, they just can't handle your pregnancy. They may be afraid it could happen to them. Your acceptance of their feelings may help them, in time, to accept yours.

Where Will I Live?

Some of you will choose to live at home, but for others that will not be an option. It's possible your parents will feel you can't stay there while you're pregnant, or you may be uncomfortable living with them. You may decide that you should stay with a relative. Or perhaps you will need to find other living arrangements altogether. Could you stay with a friend for a while? If that's unlikely, the National Citizens Concerned for Life located in Washington, D.C., has developed Crisis Pregnancy Centers throughout the United States. These centers have "shepherding homes" available for unwed mothers. The young women who live in these homes are cared for by loving, concerned house parents. The back of this book lists additional resources.

What About School?

For those of you who are still in school, you may wonder whether or not you can stay. In most schools you can continue until your seventh month, after which you may be able to switch to homebound tutoring. It might be an option to be tutored at home earlier if you wish.

There are also schools just for pregnant young women. In some states they are called Continuing Education Centers, and they differ from regular high school. The curriculum has practical, realistic options for pregnant students. There are classes in counseling for career development, homemaking, prenatal care, and family life. These centers allow plenty of opportunity for peer interaction. The program lasts about sixteen weeks, with classes held Monday through Friday, six hours daily. They offer an intensive program of academic and personal guidance. At many of the centers, expectant fathers and parental involvement are included.

If you are in college, you should be able to continue your schedule. You may wish to discuss this with your advisor. If you are working, you need to look into whether or not you are eligible for paid maternity leave, insurance, and health benefits.

In this chapter we have tried to answer some immediate questions that concern you. Our next consideration is to help you think about your options.

5.
What Are My Options?

As a pregnant single, you will want to look at all the options available to you and your child. Each option is presented here briefly, then explored in more detail later.

Do You Want to Be a Single Parent?

The everyday realities of single parenting can be better understood by reading literature on this subject. Visit your library and ask one of the staff to help you locate some books on this topic. One particularly valuable book is *The Single Parent Experience* by Carole Klein.[1]

Most crisis pregnancy centers have group sessions for new and prospective single parents. Try to attend a few of their meetings. By carefully listening to others share their joys, problems, and feelings, you can gain a better perspective on this issue. Other new mothers may present ideas, problems, or possibilities you hadn't previously considered.

[1](New York: Avon Books, 1978).

Do You Plan to Marry?

If you and the father of your baby have thought about marriage, consider that many couples who feel they *have* to get married do not "live happily ever after." Currently almost 75 percent of teen marriages end in divorce. "When pregnancy is the major reason for marriage, the failure rate goes up to 90%."[2]

However, maybe both of you consider yourselves ready to live by the marriage vows. If this is true, there are benefits to be gained by seeking premarital counseling. Otherwise, talk with a professional at any agency specifically designed to help you and your child.

Have You Considered Adoption?

Releasing your child for adoption may be a tough alternative to consider. The birth father, and maybe even your parents, should certainly be part of the counseling procedure for this issue. Seeking updated information about adoption will be extremely important in making a planned, unhurried decision.

Each of the three options is difficult, and one won't be any easier than the others. Any decision you make will require a sacrifice. When you think about your options, remember that everyone's welfare should be considered.

Thinking Things Through

Do you really have a choice? You may feel there is only one alternative for you. Not so! Allow yourself to

[2]Regis Walling, *When Pregnancy Is a Problem* (St. Meinrad, Ind.: Abbey Press, 1980), 68.

brainstorm. The choices may appear inappropriate to you, but evaluate them anyway. You do have a minimum of two alternatives: you can either keep the baby, or place him for adoption.

Would you set aside a period of time each week to concentrate first on one option? Then spend an equal amount of time thinking about each of the others. Write down the pros and cons of each. Also list the changes or plans you'd choose to make for your own life with any one of the three decisions. A sample form is included on the next page.

Although your final decision shouldn't actually be made until *after* the baby is born, it's best if you can come to a tentative conclusion two months before delivery. If you wait until the last minute, you'll feel pressured.

Do you know someone who's been pregnant and in a similar situation? Perhaps she's trying to influence you to make the exact choice she made. Don't buy it! Her decision was made on the basis of *her* circumstances. Yours needs to be based on your own experiences and goals. Each of us is unique. It's important you make the choice right for *you*.

How do people make good choices? Where do they begin?

As you are able to view your problem more objectively, you will be equipped to make a good decision. The next chapter is designed to help you with the decision-making process.

Option #1		Option #2		Option #3	
Pros	Cons	Pros	Cons	Pros	Cons

6.
How Do I Make a Good Decision?

There are now two lives to consider. The decision you make in the next few months will affect both of you for the rest of your lives. Sound frightening? If your choice is based solely on emotions, it can be.

Look at some of the decisions you've made in the past. Did you avoid the issue? Procrastinate? This is definitely one time that won't be possible. You can put it off for a few months, but not forever. Maybe you're the kind of person who sifts through all the possibilities, then stands firm. Or perhaps you're the kind who impulsively changes her mind from day to day.

It is dangerous to form your conclusion right away and then spend a lot of time justifying it. Unfortunately some young women have tunnel vision. Their decisions are already made, and they refuse to look at other alternatives. Frequently what happens is that they end up changing their decisions at the last minute. The best choice will be one that *solves* more problems than it creates and the one most agreeable with your lifestyle.

Questions to Ask Yourself:

Am I an impulsive person?
Must I have the solution right away?

Am I impatient?

Do I deal with the problem head-on?

Do I avoid the issue?

Do I blame others?

Do I believe that people do not approve of anything I do?

Do I expect or allow others to make decisions for me?

How much risk and uncertainty can I tolerate?

Am I a perfectionist? Must everything be just right?

Am I pretty good at predicting outcomes?

Am I an optimist, or a pessimist?

Answering these questions honestly will give you an idea of how you handle decision–making. It *is* possible to make wise decisions if you know the steps to follow.

How to Make a Good Decision:

1. Identify problem.
2. List alternative courses of action.
3. Gather information helpful in reaching decision.
4. Consider consequences of each alternative.
5. Consider risks in making this decision.
6. Study your values in relation to how you make a decision and carry it out.
7. Reach a conclusion *you* believe is best.

Your Situation Today

What would happen if you took no positive steps to decide what to do about your baby? Here is what happened to one young woman who did exactly that:

Heather, age sixteen, recognized her missed periods, but just blamed it on being irregular. When she started to gain weight, she told herself she was eating too much ice cream. Heather found every excuse to deny reality and actually talked herself out of the possibility of being pregnant.

She kept going out with friends to dances, continued her gymnastic lessons, and wore tight pants. Subconsciously she knew she was pregnant, but wouldn't allow herself to think about, much less discuss, the issue.

Finally Heather's mother questioned her. Although Heather denied any problem, her mother soon suspected the truth and took her daughter to a crisis pregnancy center. One month later Heather had the baby. This denial made it extremely difficult for Heather. Not only did she have to make a hurried decision, but she also had to face abruptly all the hormonal and emotional changes that occur during and after pregnancy.

Considering two lives she was now responsible for, Heather had no information on which to base her decision as she lay in the hospital bed.

You, on the other hand, can take control of your situation right now. Think about some decisions you've made before. Which classes did you decide to take and why? Did you choose to enroll in driver's education or wait another year? What kind of summer jobs did you apply for? Why? Did you take definite control, or just let events carry you along?

Pressures From Others

Will you come to your decision because you feel it's what someone else wants you to do? Or will you make your decision based on your own thoughts and feelings? Take a sheet of paper and list all the important people in your life. Beside each name write what they think you should do and why. How important is this person's opinion to you? The following story illustrates what can happen when a young woman considers the opinion of someone else more important than her own.

Rachel, age 30, is an independent career woman who was busy climbing the corporate ladder. She initially wanted to place her baby for adoption. Rachel felt unready to be a mother and had many personal goals left to fulfill. However, when she told her mother—who had seven children of her own—her mom exclaimed, "Oh no! You can't give away my grandchild!" This thought stayed with Rachel throughout her pregnancy, and not having her mother's support was difficult. In fact, it was too tough. So, wanting to please her mother, she kept the baby.

This decision divided the family because Rachel's father had a hard time accepting the circumstances.

Are You in Touch With Your Feelings?

Allow yourself to put your feet up. Sit back and daydream. What was life like one year ago? Was your hair in the same style as now? Did you have the same interests and activities? Who were your friends back then? How did you spend your time? What was important to you? What were your goals?

Now move into the present. How has the picture changed? Do you feel any different? What is important to you now? What occupies most of your time? Who do you consider your friends to be today? What are your plans for the future? Perhaps fifteen-year-old Jennifer's story will illustrate the changes that can take place in a year.

Twelve months ago Jennifer was interested in Tom. Now she considers him immature, a loser. Jennifer used to collect slogan buttons, wore knickers, and enjoyed wearing fake tattoo hearts on the side of her face. Her reading material consisted of romance stories. Looking back on these activities, she thinks to herself, "How infantile!"

Last year Jennifer wanted to be an airline stewardess. This year she seriously considered attending Juilliard School of Music. That is, until she became pregnant. Obviously her goals, if not completely changed, will at least need to be shelved for a while.

Jennifer has a lot of growing up to do. A lot of changes have occurred in her life as a result of turning fifteen and becoming pregnant. How she feels now, compared with how she'll feel at age twenty-one, is like comparing apples and bananas. With a counselor's help, Jennifer sees that although she'll feel different at twenty-one, the decision she makes today will forever affect her future.

Identifying Your Goals

What are your goals in regard to education or career? Have you thought about a vocational or technical school? Or is it more realistic to study for your Graduation Equivalency Diploma? Maybe you plan to attend college, or perhaps you are striving for an advancement in your present job.

What about a family? Do you want marriage? Children? Or have you decided to remain single?

Have you thought about goals concerning your personal growth? Maybe you want to read fifty books a year, or travel to several cities or other countries. Would you choose to take swimming, tennis, racquetball, or aerobics classes?

Your financial picture needs to be addressed as well.

Will you stay above the poverty level? Be able to afford your own apartment or buy new furniture? What about a down payment for a home or a ten-acre farm?

How would the responsibilities of parenthood affect your pursuit of these objectives?

Outside Counseling

It helps to have an objective person guide you through your decision-making process. Sometimes when we have difficult choices to make, we'd like to avoid the subject as Heather did. Many times it takes another person to force us to look at the important issues.

There are people specially trained to assist you in making arrangements for your best possible care and to help you prepare for the future. Local crisis pregnancy centers and agencies are available to help you. (A list of resources is at the back of this book.) The services provided through these centers can be received for little or no charge.

At these centers you will find people who care about your well-being and that of your baby. They may be called counselors, advocates, or social workers. Your chats with a counselor will provide a way for you to talk through solutions. Through her care and concern, she will give you the opportunity to take a look at your situation and the changes you want to make for a happier future. She can also help you gauge your readiness for parenting.

Here are a few remarks from young women who have been helped by visiting with someone at a crisis pregnancy center:

Beth: "The counselor was great. She was sensitive, yet helped me make my own decision without giving her opinion on what to do."

Jackie: "My social worker was a real help. I didn't know where else to turn, but I came to her and found acceptance and support."

Ann: "They had good suggestions. I like the way they took all the time necessary; I never felt rushed."

Denise: "They supported me a great deal without being pushy or overbearing."

Laura: "Instead of taking control of my life, the counselor allowed me to have control."

As these comments suggest, when you meet with a counselor, she can give you insight, provide a list of helpful resources, and lend you moral support. Just as important, she can serve as a mediator between you and your parents, or between you and your baby's father.

She can also counsel you about personal problems apart from plans for the baby. Depending on your needs, she can assist in obtaining financial aid, medical care, prenatal and childbirth education, and if necessary, housing, maternity clothes, and transportation.

On the next few pages there are some activity sheets for you to complete. You may want to do them once now, then again with an objective, concerned counselor.

To Help You in Your Decision Making:

The following list of words describes various kinds of feelings. Put an X beside the words that describe you when you think about releasing your baby for adoption. *Circle* the words that describe your feelings when you think about raising your child.

anxious	deserted	joyful
fearful	upset	depressed
excited	terrific	tense
elated	loving	free
happy	manipulated	unloving
lonely	content	sad
relieved	peaceful	mean
embarrassed	locked-in	fulfilled

You may also find it helpful to keep a diary or journal of your thoughts and feelings.

List all the problems you could have as you raise your baby. Now list all the problems that could arise if you release your baby for adoption. Which can you better live with?

Play the role of a young woman who wants to raise her baby. Write all the convincing reasons why this is the better alternative. Now pretend you are the young woman who wants to release her baby for adoption. Write all the reasons why this is the better choice.

CONSIDER THE CHILD

In making your decision, it is hoped that you will be able to concentrate on what you'd like for your child— his emotional and physical needs, family relationships, education, and vocation.

CONSIDER YOURSELF

Motherhood is an overwhelming responsibility at times. The next chapter will help you answer the question, Am *I* prepared to be a mother?

If I Raise My Baby	If I Release My Baby

I want to raise my baby	I want to release my baby

7.
Am I Ready for Motherhood?

Do you remember your mother saying in an exasperated tone, "Just wait till you have children of your own!"? Perhaps you tried to tease her out of whatever it was that made her angry. At the same time you may have said, "Oh that's light-years off." Neither you nor your mom realized how soon those "light-years" would arrive. Let's take a look at the joys, hassles, and responsibilities in the world of parenting.

Joys

If you have an older sister or girlfriend who's had a baby, you can remember the fascination and excitement of seeing the newborn for the first time. Before the baby was born, perhaps you went to the baby shower and took note of all the darling, tiny outfits. You saw the warm, happy glow on the expectant mother's face. All eyes were focused on her; she was in the "spotlight."

These are all pleasant and wonderful things, but they last only a short time. The spotlight soon dims. Then it's time to take the baby home from the hospital. There are many joys in being a mother; yet the responsibility of a new life to care for is awesome. There are also many heartaches and headaches that go with the title "Mom."

LYNN'S STORY

A young black woman named Lynn found her child very demanding. Because she lived with her parents, Lynn thought they would provide support. Instead they offered their advice as the "only way" to raise the child. She sadly recognized the sometimes negative effect this child had on her life. Her decision to keep the baby was made in haste. She often regretted it.

If Lynn had written all her needs out on paper, it might have looked like this:

Emotional: I need to be nurtured, loved, have my self-esteem built up, live in a secure environment, and be encouraged by my parents.

Physical: I need medical attention, food, latest style in clothes, and a home in which to live.

Spiritual: Yes, I need, and I am taken to church and Sunday school and we do worship as a family. We even take time for prayer together.

On paper this would look wonderful, but the reality was different. "I was put down a lot by my father. He didn't know how to compliment, just criticize. As for a secure environment, my parents picked at each other and seemed to thrive on bickering," Lynn said.

"Concerning physical affection, I don't remember hugs from either of them. Although we went to church, the lessons didn't carry over at home. I felt guilty about thinking they were hypocrites."

As Lynn took a good look at her situation, plus the added responsibility of her new baby, she finally realized her decision to keep the child was negatively affecting her emotions and ultimately her entire life. However, no one could tell her this when she chose to keep her baby. Lynn never realized that she would encounter so much stress.

Measure Your Stress

"Stress experts have come up with the Stress Index Chart. 'Life change unit points' were assigned to typical life events. See for yourself where you stand. Add the points to get your score. If you score less than 150, you're doing well; between 150 and 300 you probably have too much stress in your life. And because stress causes physical illness, if you score over 300 points it can mean you're headed for a major health change."[1]

WHAT ABOUT YOU?

As the chart shows, definite adjustments are required in motherhood. The manner in which you handle these changes will depend on your physical and emotional health, plus the support you receive from family and concerned loved ones. Your own needs will be great, but you may find most of your attention focused on the care of your child.

[1]Jan Markell and Jane Winn, *Overcoming Stress* (Wheaton, Ill.: Victor Books, 1982), 90–91.

THE STRESS OF ADJUSTING
TO CHANGE*

Rank	Event	Stress Points
1	Death of spouse	100
2	Divorce	73
3	Marital separation	65
4	Jail term	63
5	Death of close family member	63
6	Personal injury or illness	53
7	Marriage	50
8	Fired from job	47
9	Marital reconciliation	45
10	Retirement	45
11	Change in health of family member	44
12	Pregnancy	40
13	Sexual difficulties	39
14	Gain of new family member	39
15	Business readjustment	39
16	Change in financial state	38
17	Death of close friend	37
18	Change of work	36
19	Change in number of marital arguments	35
20	Mortgage over $10,000	31
21	Foreclosure of mortage or loan	30
22	Change in responsibility at work	29
23	Son or daughter leaving home	29
24	Trouble with in-laws	29
25	Outstanding personal achievement	28
26	Spouse begins or stops work	26
27	Beginning or end of school	26
28	Change in living conditions	25
29	Revision of personal habits	24
30	Trouble with boss	23

*From *Overcoming Stress* by Jane Markell and Jane Winn (Victor Books, 1982), 90–91.

31	Change in work hours or conditions	20
32	Change in residence	20
33	Change in schools	20
34	Change in recreation	19
35	Change in church activities	19
36	Change in social activities	18
37	Mortgage or loan less than $10,000	17
38	Change in sleeping habits	16
39	Change in number of family get-togethers	15
40	Change in eating habits	15
41	Vacation	13
42	Christmas	12
43	Minor violations of the law	11

YOUR CHILD'S NEEDS

Let's pretend for a moment that you can see into the future. What do you imagine for your child at the following ages? What would his needs be at each age?

Birth: Needs:

Six years old: Needs:

Twelve years old: Needs:

Fifteen years old: Needs:

Nineteen years old: Needs:

Imagine Yourself As a Parent

What do you think parenting will be like? Do you feel it will mean having someone always there to love you? Are you excited at the prospect of being able to experience the exciting way a child grows? Will parenting give purpose to your life? Will you be able to discipline your child when he disobeys or throws a tantrum? Do you imagine you will lose a lot of freedom? Will you feel trapped? These questions point out the appealing and unappealing aspects of parenting.

APPEALING VS. UNAPPEALING

In the first column list the things you are looking forward to in raising your baby. In the second, list what you don't look forward to. This may be difficult. Think back to some of the experiences your parents had with you as you were growing up. Your relationship with your child may differ, but there are no "perfect" parent-child relationships. There are happy and sad occasions in all families.

Appealing	Unappealing

Now that you have looked at some of the positive and negative features of raising a child, you realize that there will be inevitable adjustments. So you won't have a lot of distasteful surprises down the road, ask yourself the following questions: (Write your answers on a separate sheet of paper.)

A Change for the Better?

—What do I want out of life for myself? What do I think is important?

—Can I handle a child and a job, or school, at the same time?

—Am I ready to give up the freedom to do what I want to do when I want to do it?

—Can I afford to support a child?

—Do I want to raise a child in my neighborhood, or will I be financially able to move?

—How will a child interfere with my growth and development?

—Will my child change my educational plans?

—Am I willing to give at least eighteen years of my life to being responsible for a child's well-being?

After pondering these questions you can understand some of the changes that will occur in your lifestyle. You may be better able to relate to the following story:

A DEFINITE CHANGE IN JAN'S LIFESTYLE

Jan was used to getting up at 6:30, eating a light breakfast of toast and apple juice, or sometimes nothing at all, and then going off to work at the drug store. She sometimes resented her low-paying job, but as a drop-out she knew she couldn't do much better until she got her G.E.D. Her life was fairly predictable and routine. Then it changed.

"I couldn't believe all the adjustments I had to make when I brought Susie home from the hospital," Jan said. "Thanks to my parents' willingness to baby-sit, I still worked at the drugstore. But my sleep patterns sure got weird! Two o'clock in the morning is not exactly my shining hour. Susie is a good baby—no colic or anything like that—but for one so tiny, she sure wears me out! It was my choice to raise her, and I'm not sorry. But I never knew I would be so tired! I'm learning fast about the 'joys of motherhood.' No matter what, though, I'm determined to be a good parent."

Types of Parents

Parents come in all sizes, shapes, and personalities. You have probably encountered friends whose parents treated them quite differently from the way yours treated you. Some were lenient, others strict. Some were fun-loving, active parents, while some seemed old and tired all the time. Some are generous, others frugal. While Sally's parents attended every musical, sports, or dramatic event she was part of, Betty's parents never seemed to care whether she was even in school. They were too involved in their own problems.

Reflect on the kinds of parents you've met. Ask yourself what kind of parent you will be. Consider these questions:

AM I READY TO PARENT?

—Do I like children? What kind of experience have I had with them?

—Do I communicate easily?

—How do I express affection?

—Will I have enough patience to raise a child?

—Can I tolerate noise and confusion?

—Can I handle disrupted schedules?

—How do I release my anger? If I lost my temper, is it possible I might abuse my child?

—What does discipline mean?

—Can I set limits, yet give some freedom too?

—Do I want a perfect child?

—How do I get along with my parents?

—What will I do to avoid the mistakes my parents made?

—Do I enjoy the activities children can do?

—Do I expect my child to achieve things I didn't achieve?

—Will I want my child to keep me from being lonely in my old age?

—By having a child, will I show others how mature I am?

—Do I expect my child to make my life happy?

One thing that *can* add happiness to your life is the loving support and availability of those closest to you.

"Help! I Need Somebody!"

There's an old Beatles tune that says, "I get by with a little help from my friends." As an unmarried mother, you are going to want more than a *little* help from your friends and family. Now is the time to consider what support will actually be available when you bring your baby home. Many friends have good, worthwhile

Name: I Can Count on Them for:

1.

2.

3.

4.

5.

6.

7.

intentions; yet somehow those intentions never quite become reality.

One unwed mother actually asked her closest friends what each one would do to help her. Although some half-hearted efforts were attempted, only one out of nine friends came through as she had specifically promised.

Think of some ways relatives and friends can help you. Consider the matters of baby-sitting, helping with laundry or grocery shopping, finances, or just plain friendship. List the ones who will accept you and your baby. After each name, describe the way each person could help.

Make Room for Baby

A baby, *your* baby—a tiny bundle of flesh and bone—is a miniature human life. Yet so small, he needs many things to make his life comfortable. This section is designed to help you make room for baby.

QUESTIONS TO CONSIDER:

1. What do I need in a layette; and where will I get it?
2. How many diapers and how much formula will I need in a week?
3. How much money do I need to supply my baby's necessities?
4. What baby furniture do I need, and how can I get it?
5. Who will take care of my baby when I'm in school or at work?

6. How much does day-care cost, and what will it provide?
7. Who will furnish medical care for my baby, and what kind of care will he need?
8. How many hours can I spend each day with my baby?

WHERE WILL WE LIVE?

Where you live will depend on your age and family support. Some young women choose to live away from their parents. Because they become mothers themselves, they think it's best to live elsewhere. Two mothers in the same home can seem like one too many.

Mary decided to move out of her parents' home. She was eighteen and had recently delivered her baby. These are some of the arrangements she needed to make:

—Where is my source of income?
—How much can I afford for an apartment?
—How will I find one?
—What furniture will I need, and how do I obtain it?
—What else will I need for the apartment?
—How much money will I need each week to supply my personal needs?
—How much can I afford for utilities?

Mary had a lot to think about. You will too. It's better to try to answer these questions now. You don't want to be unprepared at the last minute.

On the other hand, many young women choose to remain at home. Cathy wanted to stay in her parents' house so she could finish her last year of high school. Cathy also had three brothers and sisters who lived at home. In planning for the baby, she had many things to discuss with her family:

—What part of the house would she and the baby stay in?

—How did the rest of her family feel about her and the baby?

—What were potential areas of conflict, and how could they be resolved?

—How could Cathy contribute to the monthly household expenses?

—Would Cathy be expected to pay rent and help with the baby's expenses?

—How would her family participate in the care of the baby?

—Could she expect free baby-sitting services? What about laundry, feeding, changing?

—How would Cathy feel when other members of the family disciplined her child?

—What about her situation in terms of dating, curfew, and personal freedom?

—Would Cathy's living arrangements meet her own needs for both structure and freedom?

The questions that Mary and Cathy had to deal with may overwhelm you. If you choose to raise your baby, however, they must be answered. Providing for a child is expensive. Our next chapter will help you to determine the costs of this challenge.

8.
Money Matters

According to a report in the April 1985 issue of *Business Week*, "Forecasters say (American) parents will spend $20 billion on children in 1990, $11 billion on clothes alone.

"When Ginny and David Crockett of suburban Philadelphia planned for the arrival of their first child, Andrew, nearly two years ago, they imagined some of the changes the baby would bring. They considered the 2:00 a.m. feeding, the visits to the pediatrician, and the general upheaval in their lives. What they didn't anticipate was the cost.

By the time Andrew enters kindergarten, he will have cost his parents more than $21,000 for goods and services, many of which—disposable diapers and organized day care, for example, barely existed when the Crockettes were growing up.

"Those dollar estimates are not exact for all families, but they do serve a purpose. The progression of childcare expenses contains a host of real-life lessons for young parents and anyone contemplating family life."

Maybe you don't expect to use disposable diapers or organized day-care. In fact, that far-off time is hard to imagine when your baby isn't born yet. But if you do choose to raise your child, there still are some financial matters to consider.

In your opinion, which of the following are necessary, and which are optional?

Apartment (rent & deposit)	Electricity & deposit
Phone & deposit	Clothing for self
Clothing for baby	Food for self
Food for baby	Eating out
Recreation/social life	Health insurance
Car insurance	Transportation
Savings	Personal needs
Medical (eyeglasses, etc.)	Child care
Gifts	Church

What Is All This Going to Cost Me?

Sarah, aged nineteen, had a good job at the telephone company. During her pregnancy, she lived at home. In her fifth month she made the decision to move out after her baby was born. Through Mrs. Adams, her counselor at a crisis pregnancy center, Sarah was able to take a good look at all that moving involved. First the counselor advised Sarah to look through newspaper want ads, call rental agencies, talk to people at her church, and pick up some apartment guides that were available at the bank.

"I'm so thankful my counselor was there to help me sort through my living arrangements. She suggested places to look for housing I wouldn't have known or thought about," Sarah said.

Next, after Sarah had looked at several possibilities,

she and Mrs. Adams listed the locations and what each would cost. Seen on paper, it was much easier to choose where the best place would be for Sarah to live with her baby.

"After I made my decision to move into a cute little apartment not far from my work, my counselor talked with me about furniture for my apartment."

"Sarah, it's important to think about the kind of furnishings you need for you and the baby," Mrs. Adams said. She suggested that Sarah visit the Salvation Army Thrift Store, Goodwill Stores, and garage sales for good baby items, and to ask her friends and relatives if they had any items they no longer used. Sarah skimmed newspaper advertisements for furniture store sales and carefully read the want ads for bargains in kitchen equipment and linens.

"Then my counselor discussed the cost of utilities with me," Sarah remembered. "Mrs. Adams suggested I call and find out the cost of having a phone installed, what the monthly costs are, and what kind of deposit they wanted. I did the same thing with the electric company, asking for an estimate of monthly charges, their hook-up fee, and the deposit required on my one-bedroom apartment.

"Our next topic was food costs and clothing. Mrs. Adams told me that getting all this stuff down on paper would help me budget my money better." Her counselor helped her estimate the monthly food bills. Sarah planned to breast-feed her baby, so the cost of infant formula wasn't included for the first several months.

"I did need to think about what clothes in my wardrobe would have to be replaced in the next six months and budget money for that," Sarah explained. "Also, Mrs. Adams gave me a list of nursery and layette items, then helped me write a list of what I needed."

Layette and Nursery Needs

CLOTHING

2 dozen cloth diapers *or*
2 packages disposable diapers
6 cotton shirts
3–5 sleepers
4 waterproof panties (if using cloth diapers)
8 safety pins, double-locking heads (if using cloth diapers)
Sweater set
2 blanket sleepers
3–5 receiving blankets
Booties or socks

FEEDING EQUIPMENT

If breast-feeding, 2 or more bottles for water and juice
If bottle-feeding, 8 bottles
Pre-sterilized, disposable nurser kit
8 nipples and caps
Bottle and nipple brushes
4 bibs

BED AND BATH

Bathinette or portable baby bath
Toiletries: soap or liquid cleanser, lotion, powder,

cotton swabs, cream, petroleum jelly, moist towelettes, shampoo, ointment
   2–3 crib blankets
   3 fitted sheets
   1 small waterproof pad

FOR OUTINGS

Stroller
Car seat
Bunting or pram suit
Insulated bottle and diaper bag

BASIC NURSERY NEEDS

Crib
Mattress
Crib bumper
Chest of drawers
Dressing or changing table
Diaper pail
Infant seat
Rectal thermometers
Record book
Nursery lamp
Crib mobile
Toys

Later Additions

Playpen and pad
Portable stroller
Baby walker, jumper, or exerciser
Portable baby swing

Toilet seat or chair
Toy box
Table and chair set
Safety gates and latches
Children's books

Medical Care

After attending her baby shower and buying a few new things, Sarah went to the same places she had explored for her furniture.

"With food, housing, and clothes out of the way, I had to think about my baby's medical needs," Sarah said. "Mrs. Adams recommended I read some books on this subject, then write down the necessary medical care my baby would require for the first six months. This included a call placed to my local public health office to find out immunization schedules, locations, and costs for a baby." She also called her family doctor's office to ask the approximate expense involved for well-baby care in the first six months.

"Naturally I talked with my health insurance company to find out what kind of coverage my baby and I had, and to see what else they had available," Sarah stressed. "After getting that information, I was better able to estimate my medical expenses and what would, and wouldn't be covered per month.

"My list of personal needs was a bit easier to do because I had already started to keep track about three months ago. I kept a pretty thorough run-down of items like toilet paper, aspirin, perfume, tampons, toothpaste, and cosmetics. It didn't take long to fill out this sheet my counselor gave me:

My Personal Needs: What They Cost:

_____   _____

_____   _____

_____   _____

_____   _____

_____   _____

_____   _____

Another part of child-rearing Sarah contemplated was who would care for her baby while she worked. Sarah learned that she needed to check various local day-care centers to get their costs of care and find out exactly what they provided. She found some in the telephone book and newspaper ads and went to visit them. Her counselor told Sarah it would also be wise to ask some of her friends and relatives their hourly baby-sitting rates.

The last item they discussed was transportation. Mrs. Adams asked Sarah to estimate her cost for transportation per month, then to consider available alternatives—such as mass transit.

The counselor finally gave her a budget exercise sheet to fill out. "It was a pain to do," Sarah explained, "but it did help me see where my money would go each month."

Like Sarah, we have included an exercise sheet here for you to complete. If you can get some idea now of what you'll need to purchase each month, it won't seem like such a shock later on. Better yet, you'll have time to get ready and prepare for expenses.

Keep in mind that the time you spend contemplating

WHERE HAS ALL THE MONEY GONE?

Necessary Expenditures: Costs Per Month:

_____   _____

_____   _____

_____   _____

_____   _____

_____

                                 Total: _____

Optional Expenditures: Costs Per Month:

_____   _____

_____   _____

_____   _____

_____   _____

                                 Total: _____

Monthly Income: _____

Subtract Total of Necessary Items: _____

Subtotal: _____

Subtract Optional Items: _____

Balance: _____

your budget will be worth it. Writing the figures down now will save you money and also a lot of headaches later.

AFDC and WIC

It's important to know there is help available through the Department of Human Services with a program called Aid to Families with Dependent Children. But please be aware that if you walk the AFDC route, paternity will need to be established, therefore giving the father responsibility as well as rights.

There is also the WIC program, which is designed to help improve the diet of pregnant women during the critical times that the baby needs nutritious foods. When a woman participates in the WIC program, she not only learns which foods will help her have a healthy baby, but she can receive many of these foods as well. All free of charge. To receive WIC benefits, the woman must have a health need that nutrition, education and WIC foods can help. Needs are determined by medical history. To find out if you qualify, call your local health department.

If you want to continue your education or pursue job training, AFDC may be able to assist you with the financing of child care. Many young, unwed mothers find they need financial help. For instance, in just one county in Tennessee it was discovered that over 70 percent of welfare recipients were teens when they bore their first child.

While it can be expensive to raise a child, it can also be rewarding. The next chapter will introduce you to four young women who each looked for different "rewards" in motherhood.

9.
Checking My Motives

Unwed mothers have various reasons for deciding to keep and raise their children. Now is a good time to examine your motives. See if you can identify with any of these young women.

Kelly

Kelly, aged seventeen, totally expected her child to fulfill her own desperate need to be loved. "When I was thirteen, my father left us. Mom had to hold down two jobs to support me and my two sisters. She didn't have much time left over for affection," Kelly related.

This was Kelly's second pregnancy. After she gave up her first baby, she suffered from a sense of loss and loneliness.

"When I got pregnant this time, I thought now I'd have someone to really love and someone who will love me. I believed I was ready to have another one, settle down, and make a good home. I felt the baby could give me just what I needed.

"The first six weeks with my son were okay. My mom would come over and all my friends wanted to see the baby and hold him. The newness of it all was exciting! For the first time, I found a purpose in life and really thought someone needed me. All my life I just wanted to be needed."

Kelly's son is now two years old. "I do love him, but I'm finding out it's more than a give-and-take situation. I'm giving, giving, giving, and he's taking, taking, taking. Sometimes I feel drained, with no energy, and very little love to give.

"He tends to be demanding at times. I'll never forget the last time we went to the grocery store. What a scene! My son stood in the aisle with three bags of candy in his arms. One bag was halfway open and he refused to let go. I stood there afraid to take the bags away for fear he'd have a screaming tantrum. How embarrassing! What happened is, I ended up buying all three bags.

"I recognize that my child's needs are important, but it's hard to be loving and give of myself when I got so little attention in my younger years. There's so much I need for me. I know he needs discipline, activities to keep him busy, and loving attention, but I'm finding it an endless effort because I have some needs too."

Kelly looked reflective. "It's real nice when he's sitting in my lap. We cuddle together and rock in the chair. But sometimes he grabs my lipstick when I'm not looking and smears it on the wall. Then it's not so nice."

Carol

Carol is a mature nineteen-year-old who has been brought up in a positive, loving family environment. "My reason for keeping the baby is that I felt I could parent her responsibly. *I* wanted to be the one to help my child develop physically, emotionally, spiritually, and I wanted to work hard toward her overall well-being."

Carol is realistic and recognizes that there will be ups as well as downs with the responsibility of mother-hood. Carol is emotionally mature enough not to depend on the child to make her life happy.

"My own needs are being met through a great family support system. My baby's father is no longer involved, but I have a strong faith in God and can rely on Him rather than myself," she said. "I am highly motivated to parent. And one thing that really helped me was to read some good books on child care and parenting."

Carol's motive was basically good. She felt she could be a good parent, and she had the self-confidence necessary to carry this out. She knew she could give and didn't need to receive a lot from her baby. Carol has a good self-image. Her strength comes from within, and she also relies on God's power to help her.

Ann

Ann's attitude was, "It's my child and no one else is going to raise him. I got myself into this, now I'll just have to suffer." Her family had told her repeatedly, "You must keep your child. There's no other way!"

A neighbor of Ann's had placed her baby for adoption. When Ann's mother heard this, she was horrified: "How in the world could she just up and give away her little baby!"

Ann got the message. According to her mother, adoption was *not* the thing to do. Her native American culture said, "You don't give away your own flesh and blood. It's taboo."

For Ann, the only option that seemed possible was to keep the baby. Her values suggested she was good if she kept the baby, bad if she released him. As a result, her goals and ambitions were put on hold.

It didn't take long before she developed resentment toward the whole situation. "My family is well off and have promised to provide the finances, but I feel locked in, like this is my lot in life," Ann said. "I'm graduating in a couple months and would love to go on to college, to be free and do what I want to do. But that's out for the time being. I guess I decided to keep the baby because I never saw any other choice."

Ellen

Ellen based her decision to keep the child on a sincere hope that the baby would force the baby's father to continue their relationship. "I believed that once Charlie watched me go through childbirth and actually saw the baby, he would realize my love for him and give me what I wanted, a wedding. I counted on the delivery room experience to convince him we should marry.

"I was stunned when he still wanted me to place the baby. He said he didn't feel we were financially ready. Charlie didn't want to think about settling down or handling the responsibility. He said we'd get married later on. That was hard to take. I felt like telling him he could either take me and the baby *now* or forget it. It was like a slap in the face. I just couldn't understand how he would want to continue our relationship, yet not include our baby."

Ellen never told Charlie that she'd made any decision. "Knowing how bad he wanted me to place, yet at the same time thinking he wouldn't be able to resist his own son, I kept quiet and hoped he'd change his mind," Ellen stated.

"A couple days after the birth, Charlie came to see me at the hospital. My parents told him about my decision. He didn't show any emotion, but I sensed he was upset. After my folks left, he really let me have it! 'Ellen, I've told you over and over from the very beginning! Can't you get it through your head? I will not marry you if you keep that kid!' With that he stomped out of my hospital room.

"Although he'd made it clear where he stood, I refused to give up hope," Ellen related. "After I took the baby home, I figured when he came to visit me, he'd have to see the baby too. Then he'd understand I was being a good mother to his son. He'd see me hold our baby and watch me take care of him. I was determined to prove to him that I could be, not only a good mother, but also a good wife."

You may have the same motive that Ellen had. The next chapter will help you test your readiness for marriage and give you guidelines to prepare yourself for the big step down the aisle.

10.
Will I Say "I Do"?

Marriage often seems like the best solution to the problem pregnancy, the easiest way out. Your womanly instincts may tell you that babies belong within "the holy bonds of matrimony." Perhaps you believe it wouldn't look right without a father around the house. Gossip about your situation may pressure you to marry. But don't let the tongue-waggers make your decision for you.

On the other hand, if you are ready to settle down, this alternative can be wonderful for all concerned. Nevertheless, it takes two committed people to make it work.

"In marriage you commit yourself to a stable and lasting union with another person. This union should help you grow as a person and be a source of happiness and contentment in life. It should also help the growth of your spouse and should provide a stable, secure environment for rearing children. For you, this means the child already growing inside you, as well as other children you may have."[1]

Let's examine what it takes to make this solution one

[1] Ida Critelli and Tom Schick, *Unmarried and Pregnant: What Now?* (Cincinnati: St. Anthony Messenger Press, 1977), 32.

that will work, and also help you determine whether or not your relationship has the right characteristics to make it last.

Is He Your "Prince Charming"?

Have you ever dreamed about the ideal time and perfect person to settle down with and start a family? When is that ideal time? What would the father of your baby be like?

Theresa shared with a support group of pregnant young women that she had always dreamed of beginning her family after she and her husband had some time to "just be together and get to know each other."

"I never really wanted to get married until my late twenties," Theresa said. "I felt I wanted to experience and savor life before settling down." She shared dreams of travel to Europe, then of time spent raising her horses, which she had entered in shows for several years. However, the truth is that she's seventeen and pregnant, and the boy she has dated for the past five months wants to marry her.

Theresa's dreams contrast sharply with her current situation. "After thinking it through, I feel I can sacrifice my 'ideal' and commit myself instead to raising my child," she said. "My dreams of travel and horses will have to wait. What still concerns me, though, is whether I want to work at being Steve's wife for the rest of my life."

Steve doesn't exactly have all the qualities she looks for in a husband; but after all, he is the father of her child. Still, she wonders if she can put away the hope of marrying her "perfect dream man."

Which Qualities Are Important?

Theresa felt that the most important quality she wanted in her man was the ability to accumulate wealth. "Steve makes five dollars an hour right now. He assures me that with raises over the next few years, his paycheck will be sufficient. I guess I was looking for more than just 'sufficient.' I want a large house in the country, a three-car garage, and a car in each stall. My dreams include a cook and live-in nanny. Oh well," she sighed. "I've always heard that money doesn't buy happiness. Now I'll have a chance to find out if that's true."

The next item Theresa looked for in a man was personality. "Steve is loaded with pizazz and has a terrific sense of humor. He is the type of person who makes you feel good just to be around him. All people get depressed once in a while, but with him he hasn't got time for that sort of sad-faced stuff. He's too busy enjoying life and all it has to offer." In this respect Steve and Theresa have much going for them.

Her man's faith was important to Theresa. "I never cared much for people who were wishy-washy about what they believe," she said. "Steve is wonderful in that department! He believes there is a God, and we've spent many hours discussing our Creator's attributes. Sometimes we visit my church; at other times we go to his. Our beliefs match perfectly, so we wouldn't have trouble in this area."

THINK IT THROUGH

Here's an exercise to give you perspective about the possibility of marriage.

Qualities of Your Current Boyfriend

1.
2.
3.
4.
5.
6.
7.

Qualities of Your "Ideal Mate"

1.
2.
3.
4.
5.
6.
7.

How do the lists compare? What qualities are lacking? Can you overlook these?

What Is Your Relationship Like?

"Love. A key ingredient—*the* ingredient—for successful marriage is love. Do you love the man you are thinking of marrying? Does he love you? Of course! Are you sure?

"You don't have to define love to experience it. Nevertheless, love is one of the hardest emotions not only to define but to recognize.

"Love is far more than the tingling feeling of another's presence, more than the ecstasy of sexual intercourse. The true extent of love is measured by one's relationship to another when the tingling stops, when the glamour and romance and thrills are interrupted by day-to-day realities, by the stresses and strains of life together."[2]

The time will come when the tingling stops. There can be sweet interludes, but it won't be all moonbeams and roses. H. Norman Wright, author of thirty-six books on marriage, says, "Most people prepare more for their driver's test than they do for marriage." To help you be prepared, now is the time when you will want to carefully consider the following questions:

1. If I weren't pregnant, would I still think of him as a possible marriage partner?
2. Do my boyfriend and I understand each other's feelings about religion, work, family, child raising, future goals? Are these feelings compatible? Are they conducive to good parenting?
3. Is sex the focal point of our relationship? Or does it include more than physical attraction?
4. Do we have common interests and hobbies?
5. How well do we communicate?
6. What attracts us to each other?
7. What are his faults and shortcomings? Can I accept these?
8. How concerned does he seem about the baby?
9. Do both of us feel the same way about wanting to parent the child?
10. How would my boyfriend contribute to the child care responsibilities?
11. How stable is our relationship?
12. How do I really feel about marriage being a commitment for life?

[2]Ibid., 33–34.

13. Will we be able to share each other unselfishly with our child?

14. Are we *both* ready to give our time and energy to raising our baby?

Heavy questions, right? But they need to be answered *MX if you're serious about marriage. There's no doubt about it. Even when a couple enters into marriage without a child to consider, there is a big adjustment to make.

Marriage Is an Adjustment

Let's return to Theresa's story. "My counselor gave me a book called *When Pregnancy Is a Problem* that really helped me see some things I hadn't thought about before. One part said, 'There are three major transitions in the lives of most people. They are changes from:

adolescence to adulthood

single life to married life

non-parenthood to parenthood.

" 'Each development requires time in itself and the completion of the previous stage. In a teenage marriage where pregnancy is involved, you must make *all* of these transitions *at one time*.'[3]

"What the book said made me realize that marriage to Steve is more than slipping rings on our fingers and calling ourselves man and wife. After the honeymoon, there would be big adjustments to make. And they'd be ones we'd have to make together, both of us going through them at the exact same time.

"After we discussed some adjustments and changes

[3]Regis Walling, *When Pregnancy Is a Problem* (St. Meinrad, Ind.: Abbey Press, 1980), 67–68.

that were bound to happen, my counselor gave me two copies of a stress chart [see page 48] and told me and Steve each to put a star by the ones that affected us. It was a painful eye-opener! Neither one of us could have guessed we'd each rack up close to 300 points!

"The next time I met with my counselor," Theresa said, "she suggested we talk about *why* I wanted to get married. Most people don't consciously think about their reasons for wanting a wedding, but in my situation, with the baby coming and all, it was very helpful to put my motives into words."

Are Your Intentions Legitimate?

Have you thought about *why* you want to get married? Is it a legitimate escape? Do you feel it will get you out of a poor family environment? Or give you a chance to develop the stable family you've longed for? As we mentioned elsewhere, "Currently between 70 and 75% of teen marriages end in divorce, and when pregnancy is *the* reason for the marriage, the failure rate is nearly 90%."[4]

Perhaps you want marriage because someone will be there to care for and love you. The truth is, we all have to find and love ourselves first before we can love others. It is a fact that we take ourselves with us wherever we go. Marriage can add to our confusion of trying to discover who we are and who we want to become.

You may have been in a relationship for years. Neither one of you are kids anymore. Now that you're pregnant, you believe the two of you will marry. Does he agree with this? Will you marry out of guilt? Do you

[4]Ibid., 68.

think marriage is the only honorable choice? Is this what you're *expected* to do? Following this line of reasoning, many couples feel trapped in their marriages. The trapped feeling can lead to anger and resentment toward your spouse. Both partners can feel a sincere sense of responsibility, yet have an underlying hostile attitude. What sometimes happens then is that the baby can become an object of resentment, even physical abuse. If you grew up in a volatile atmosphere, the chance of abuse is far greater. Most of us tend to parent the way we've been parented.

Are you marrying because of parental pressure? "There was a time when in a case of the pregnancy of an unwed woman there was only one honorable thing to do. Marriage was hastily arranged and 'they lived happily ever after.' Not always did they live 'happily,' nor do they today."[5]

Your parents may be urging you to "make it legal," to "give the baby a name." In all honesty, however, the opinions of friends and relatives are far less important than the stability—or lack of it—in a marriage. If you plan to marry, what do you expect to get out of it?

Your Marriage Expectations

Remember the movie *Blue Hawaii* starring Elvis Presley? The scene where he and his beautiful co-star float on a gorgeous flower-bedecked boat will remain one of the most romantic wedding sequences in film history.

The media are filled with fantasies of roses, orange blossoms, and moonlit nights. Of course, they conveniently hide the thorns and thunderstorms. The movie producers go to extraordinary lengths to portray love and marriage as something magic and mystical.

[5]Ibid.

It has been said that "where love is blind, marriage is a great eye-opener." Those of us who have been there commend all who are able to enter matrimony with their eyes wide open.

How do you feel about your role in marriage? Are you for the traditional role of husband bringing home the bacon and you frying it? Or do you steer toward the more modern thought of each wandering into the other's territory? Discuss this aspect with your boyfriend. You may find you are in absolute agreement. But more than likely, compromises will be needed.

Do you foresee any obstacles to the two of you marrying? What happens if both of your families are cool to the idea? Is there a problem with finances? Maybe both of you are underage. What then? Are you and your boyfriend able to handle the loss of anticipated goals? Is yours a stable relationship? Does either of you see yourself as forced into marriage? These are questions that are best to get out in the open and discussed *now*.

What benefits will marriage provide? Is it possible for three to live as cheaply as one? You would have companionship and never worry about a date. You'd have a father for the child and a husband to provide for the three of you.

If the benefits outweigh the obstacles, then marriage could be tailor-made for you. A good thing to remember is that marriage should ultimately *solve* more problems than it creates.

Then again, maybe you're not 100 percent in agreement with marriage to your baby's father. In that case, your next step is to consider the alternative of adoption.

11.
Making Plans for Adoption

Making plans to place your baby for adoption is *your* decision only—not a counselor's or an agency's or the government's. No one can force you to release your child against your will. You have the first right to parent your child. However, to make an intelligent decision, look at all the options, one of which is the tough choice of adoption.

"Your alternative, placing your baby for adoption, may involve a difficult decision. It may run counter to your very real 'mother instinct,' which will grow through the months of your pregnancy as the reality of your baby grows larger within you. But your 'mother instinct' wants what is really best for your baby.

"If you decide to place your baby, you can be confident his new parents will love him as their own. Today, adoptive parents seeking babies are far more numerous than the babies available.'"[1]

Reasons for Placing

At age nineteen, Trudy lived in a sparsely furnished, basement efficiency apartment with her two children.

[1]Ida Critelli and Tom Schick, *Unmarried and Pregnant: What Now?* (Cincinnati: St. Anthony Messenger Press, 1977), 46.

One day she called the Child Protection Agency. Her eighteen-month-old had upset her, and Trudy was afraid she would lose control. Because she had many emotional needs herself, which included a big desire to be loved and accepted, her relationships with men had not been positive. Trudy admitted that most of the reason for her anger and hot temper was due to her always trying to please others, never herself.

Trudy had a host of hostile feelings toward her newborn's father, who was not the father of her toddler. Her call to the Child Protection Agency arose out of deep concern for the welfare—even life—of her ten-day-old baby.

"I've made so many mistakes with the first child," Trudy mourned, "I don't want to make the same ones with the second baby." Her toddler was unruly and lacked discipline because Trudy felt weak and had unfulfilled desires of her own. She had been in therapy for several months.

Due to her inability to cope with the first child, Trudy's friends, family, and caseworker all supported Trudy in this decision to place her second baby for adoption.

Karen

Karen was an adopted child herself. At age seventeen, she felt that the most important thing to her was that her child have two parents. She was brought up in a nurturing home and appreciated her father and mother. Over the years they had recalled for Karen the excitement in their hearts the day they brought her home.

Karen had an older friend, aged nineteen, who kept

her little boy. Karen saw Scott as a child who had no one to go fishing or play ball with. The strain of trying to be both mom and dad, in Karen's opinion, could be exhausting.

She chose to take the focus off herself and place it on her child and his welfare. She also did not want the stigma of illegitimacy placed on her baby.

As a mature seventeen-year-old, Karen was thoughtful and always doing kind deeds for others—such as volunteer work at the local hospital. She firmly believed the greatest kindness she could give her child was to release him.

Still, her decision didn't come easily. Some of her peers at school gave her a bad time. "People came up to me in the hall and said, 'Oh, how can you do that to your baby—give it away like it's nothing—babies are just so cute and everything?' I told these kids right out that 'cute' had nothing to do with it. If they wanted 'cute,' they should buy some kind of a pet. Babies are not pets. They're people who need all the love in the world."

Karen concluded, "When I'm a parent, I want a husband and a nice place to live for my family."

Terri

"I'm too young [fourteen], and I recognize there really isn't any choice in my situation," Terri related. "My parents say I can't keep the baby, and that's the end of it. Of course, they can't force me to adopt my child out, but I still need a roof over my head.

"What am I supposed to do?" Terri questioned. "Get an apartment? Take my baby to a day-care center on my bike? Lie about my age to get a job—with absolutely no work experience?"

The concluding factor for Terri was that her parents would be unhappy if she kept the child, and most likely they would make Terri miserable too.

"I couldn't live with that," she claimed.

After her anticipated delivery, Terri will release her baby for adoption. "I dream sometimes about my boyfriend and marrying him. But who's to know if we're going to be right for each other a few years down the road? Besides, I'm only fourteen, way too young to be a wife."

Juliana

"I'm twenty-three and always thought this kind of thing happened to others," said Juliana. "I sure found out otherwise, didn't I?" She has friends who are her same age, some of whom have children and seem content. "It's not that I'm too young to keep this child; it's just that I want more than anything to see the baby raised in a two-parent family. I feel everyone deserves a mother *and* a father. I'm adopted and grateful that my birth mother allowed me to go to a loving home, complete with both parents."

Still, there are times when guilt creeps in. "I guess most anyone my age would feel guilty," she admits. "But I refuse to let guilt ruin my baby's chances of a decent home life. The way I figure it, I'll make *three* people happy."

It's Not the Easy Way Out

If you choose adoption, be prepared for grief. The separation will be painful. "We grieve the loss of any love, and all forms of loss have stages of grief in common."[2]

There is no question but that you will hurt emotionally. Placing a child for adoption is almost like a death. You *will* grieve. But your baby won't. This may sound harsh. But there's no need to feel sorry for him. He will go to a good home and be well provided for. *You* are the one who must deal with pain and loss, not the baby.

Questions and Answers About Adoption

Q.How long will it take to place my baby in an adoptive home?

A.You will not and should not sign an adoptive consent until your discharge from the hospital. With all the physical and emotional changes that follow delivery, it's important to allow yourself time to reevaluate the decision to place. Sometimes it takes a few days to recognize the reality of your baby's birth.

Before you leave the hospital, you will sign a custody release that allows the baby to be placed in a licensed foster home. You will remain the legally responsible parent until an adoptive consent is signed, or until a Termination of Parental Rights (TPR) hearing occurs. This generally takes place within three to six weeks after the baby's birth.

Q.May I name the baby?

A.Yes. The name you give the baby will go on the

[2]Ira J. Tanner, *Healing the Pain of Everyday Loss* (Minneapolis: Winston Press, 1980), 53.

original birth certificate, which you will be asked to sign during your stay in the hospital.

The father's last name can be used only with his permission, and it cannot be placed on the birth document without his signature and your permission.

Q.What if I'm not sure after I have the baby whether I want to keep or place?

A.If you are undecided, it is wise to place the baby in a licensed foster home. This gives you time to think through this important decision without making any hasty commitments you may later regret.

You will do both yourself and the baby a favor by taking this time to reevaluate and prepare for whatever option you choose. No consent for adoption will be signed until you are *positive* of your decision.

Q.May I see the baby while I'm in the hospital?

A.You maintain your full parental rights while you are there, and you may see the baby as much as you like. In *The Art of Adoption*, Linda Cannon Burgess relates this story:

> People in general and doctors in particular think social workers are cruel in advocating that an unmarried mother see her child before making a decision for adoption. They say, "If she sees the baby, she will never want to give him up." This is the very reason why I encourage mothers to see their babies before making irreversible decisions. If a mother is so uncertain that merely viewing the child would change her mind, she is not ready to relinquish him forever.

> I am reminded of a long distance phone call I received from a mother who had surrendered her baby two years before I joined the agency. She pictured her daughter wasting away in an orphanage. The mother told me that she had married and the birth of another daughter had renewed thoughts of her first. She was overwhelmed by the conviction that she had

abandoned her first child. She was unable to sleep, attend her new baby, or respond to her husband.

I told her that I knew the child had been adopted and promised to find out more. I located the young couple who had adopted the child. In compassion and goodwill for the birth mother, they gave me a detailed account of their daughter's wondrous ways, her appearance, her grace and beauty. A week later, I was able to relay to the mother all I had been told. She had already come out of her despondency with grateful relief, just to know her baby had been adopted. She asked over and over, "What does she look like?" and was pleased by the apparent resemblance to her second child. She struggled to explain: "You see, Mrs. Burgess, I never once laid eyes on my baby. I never saw her. I never held her even once."

Having lived with her baby *in utero* for nine months, having felt her turns and her thrusts, having labored and given birth to her but not to have looked at her was, for this sensitive mother, abandonment without love. If with love she had held and blessed her child, she could then have surrendered her for adoption without the burden of future guilt.[3]

So it can be good for you to see your child. However, it is also wise to set some limits on how much time you will spend with the baby. Your maternal instincts may urge you toward spending large amounts of time with him. But by doing so, you may be setting yourself up for more pain when it comes time to let go.

Perhaps you could visit the baby *only* in the nursery, rather than having him brought to your room. Many mothers who have premature infants must visit their babies in the nursery. Therefore, your behavior wouldn't be considered odd if this were your choice.

[3]Linda Cannon Burgess, *The Art of Adoption* (New York: W. W. Norton, 1981), 25.

Another possibility is to have the baby brought to your room once in the morning and then once again in the evening. Or, maybe you would prefer only to see the baby immediately following delivery, then for the last time just prior to your discharge.

Some young women do choose not to see their babies. This is a decision you must make for yourself. What may be comfortable for one may not be right for someone else.

It is helpful to know that when you arrive at the hospital, you may request *not* to be placed on the maternity floor. Depending on your temperament, you may also ask for a private room if you wish.

If you are still unsure about the importance of seeing the baby, remember that viewing the child will awaken you to the reality of the birth. It can also assist you in starting the grieving process. You need to identify the object of loss, otherwise you may remain forever in denial of the birth. Not seeing the baby will also produce unanswered questions like, "Who does he look like? Is he physically all right? What color hair does he have?"

Q.If I am a minor, do I need my parents' permission to place my child for adoption?

A.The laws vary from state to state, but in most cases, the law requires your parents' consent to the adoption if you are underage.

Q.Does the baby's father need to consent to the adoption?

A.Every attempt will be made to obtain his consent, because he has a legal right to be involved in the planning for his child. If he is a minor, a consent will also be obtained from his parents if possible.

In the event the baby's father is uncooperative and

won't sign the consent, he must at least be served legal notice of the TPR hearing. Once he has been notified, he can attend the hearing or waive his rights by not appearing.

Q. What if my child should want to find me when he is older?

A. The laws vary from state to state concerning the disclosure of information from an original birth certificate. In many states, the child may obtain this information at the age of nineteen or twenty-one, if he requests it and if the birth parent has authorized disclosure of that information.

Q. Do I have a choice about who adopts my baby?

A. Yes. Most agencies will locate an adoptive home that matches your reasonable specifications. You will be asked what qualities you're looking for in adoptive parents, such as age, religion, race, hobbies, rural/city residence, and so on.

Almost all agencies are willing to share as much non-identifying information as you would like to know about the couple. It might help to write out your specific questions about the family. Then when you meet with the social worker or counselor, she can address your concerns.

Q. How well does the agency know the adoptive parents?

A. The written adoptive application contains details like the personal history and current situation of the adoptive parents. It includes, but is not limited to, education, military service, medical history, financial status, employment history, religious affiliation, and an autobiography of personal and family history from childhood to present.

The adoptive studies generally consist of a minimum

of four interviews, the statements of six references, verification of and treatment for infertility, verification of their marriage, proof of good health, and clearance with the Bureau of Criminal Apprehension. References will be solicited from their co-workers, pastor, and family physician. If there is already a school-aged child in the home, a school report is also obtained. The interviews with the adoptive family include in-depth discussions about their marriage, their relationships with children, and their plans for good parenting.

Q. May I have direct contact with the adoptive parents?

A. In the last few years, agencies have recognized the value of a more open adoption. Prior to this there was no type of contact between birth and adoptive parents. It was believed that the less the adoptees knew, the better off they were.

Nowadays openness can range from the exchange of pictures and information through the agency for a specified number of years to even meeting with each other. The sharing of this information helps birth parents work through the grieving and loss. It can assure them that the child is happy and healthy and affirm their choice for adoption as a good one.

Sometimes a semi-open meeting can be arranged if all parties are in agreement. Generally, these meetings occur following the termination of parental rights and are on a first name basis only with no identifying information exchanged. The purpose of these meetings is to give both parties the chance to meet face-to-face. This can be an emotional experience, but usually affirms the decision and helps the birth parents and adoptive parents feel comfortable with each other. It's common for birth parents and adoptive parents to want to capture their feelings on paper.

These letters are a sample of the emotions that whirl through hearts, minds, and souls when a baby leaves his natural mother to live with his new family. Here are a few of those heartfelt letters.

EXPRESSIONS OF LOVE

Dear Adoptive Parents,

When I first became pregnant I didn't know what to do. I wanted to have an abortion, but soon realized I'd be killing a human life. I think that would have been harder to live with. Then I started to think about keeping my baby. But soon again I realized what all it would involve. I'd have to quit high school and my job. I don't want to sound selfish, but I didn't want to have to give up these things. I wanted to buy a car and go onto more schooling later. So I finally decided to place my baby for adoption.

This decision was not an easy one. I've cried over it many times. But I've learned through all my pain that I have given you a chance of a lifetime. You now have someone who means everything to you. I am positive you will love and take care of him as if he were yours through natural birth.

My memories of Josh will always be with me. He is a part of me and I'm a part of him. But I have to totally let go so that I don't feel like I'm just kidding myself, and keep hoping I'll see him again.

Someday when I need to share my feelings again, I hope you will accept my letters. I may want to write to Josh, but I'm not sure. He's yours now and I know if roles were reversed, I wouldn't want a lot of communication. I would feel like my space was being invaded.

Well I have to go to class now, so I'll end this. Please take the best care of my little sweetheart. I'll always love him as much as you both do, maybe even more. I wish you the best of luck with Joshua forever.

Love,
Joshua's Birth Mother

To Angela's New Parents,

Thank you for the wonderful letter you wrote me. It meant a lot being it's the only contact I have had with my daughter. You noted the little things about her that I noticed too . . . her brown eyes, beautiful red hair, and her alertness. Enclosed you can find a letter I have written to my little Angela. Please give it to her someday whether it be ten or twenty-one years from now.

Please never hold back the truth that I love her, because I truly do. Tell Angela I did what I did because I wanted her to have a better life than I have.

Continue to pray for me. I still have a lot of growing to do and need prayers and guidance. My counselor told me you have prayed for me faithfully. I appreciate that!

I have to say goodby now. I am praying for you, your new daughter and your lives together. I love her and I love you. I know you will take good care of her and teach Angela all about God and His love.

Sincerely,
Her Birth Mom

Dear Birth Mother,

How do we express our feelings of gratefulness? We are so thankful for the little "flower" you have so graciously given to us. Roseann is an answer to years of prayer.

Our older son feels special because he knows you wanted him to be Roseann's brother, and he is already becoming the "great protector" of his little sister.

Roseann has a winsome, cheery smile and is responsive to our voices and facial expressions. She has been given many lovely clothes and fun toys from friends and relatives. But the most precious gift has come from you. The music box that plays "Brahms Lullaby" represents your love and concern for her.

We can appreciate the difficult decision it must have been for you. Our prayers are with you as you mourn the loss and look on toward your future.

With Our Heartfelt Love,
Roseann's Chosen Family

Q. What will the adoptive parents know about me?

A. Adoption agencies furnish the prospective parents with a written description of your baby's family history, which you will supply. This includes all information they can give about you without revealing your identity. You will supply background information about yourself that includes medical history, education and employment background, and facts about family members.

Q. What will the adoptive parents tell my child about me?

A. Agencies encourage adoptive parents to use the word "adoption" occasionally in the child's presence long before he can possibly understand the meaning of this term. They tell the parents that his adoption should not be kept from him "until he is older."

There are some excellent books available for children that agencies can recommend. This reading material helps the child to understand about adoption from an early age. One of them is called *Color Me Loved*, by Carolyn Owens (Minneapolis: Bethany House, 1982). It is an activity book that parents and child can work on together.

Agencies also point out to adoptive parents that it's important to give the child as much positive information about his background as possible. Included will be the assurance that you loved him so much, you wanted to be sure he'd have a complete family who would be able to provide a loving home for him.

Q. Do I need to place my baby through an adoption agency? If I know of a couple who wants to adopt, can I place my baby with them?

A. Some states allow private adoptions. These placements are often arranged by a third party, perhaps an attorney or physician. To be certain that the placement is legal according to laws in your state, check with a licensed adoption agency, or your state department of welfare.

A distinct advantage to working with a licensed agency is that after experiencing the normal emotional swings which follow delivery, you are not placed in a position of immediately having to make a final decision regarding the baby's future. He is placed in a licensed foster home, and this allows you time to make your choice. The tentative decision you made before the baby's birth may look entirely different after he is born. Another advantage of working with an agency is, should future counseling or contact be requested, the staff will be available to assist those involved in the adoption.

Q. What is the termination hearing like?

A. A TPR hearing differs according to which state you live in, but in Minnesota the hearing is very brief, taking approximately five minutes. Usually it will be held in the judge's chambers, rather than an official courtroom. You will see a judge, but no jury.

Present at the hearing will be you, the father of the baby—if he so chooses—your parents or guardian if you are underage, and your social worker or counselor.

You have a right to be represented by an attorney,

but if you are voluntarily terminating parental rights, your social worker or agency will prepare all the legal documents. If you still want an attorney, but can't afford the cost, the county will appoint one. It is your privilege to have the assistance of an attorney, but you don't need one.

The TPR hearing is for *your* benefit. The judge wants to make sure you are not being pressured, that placing the baby is your own decision, you have had plenty of time to decide, and you understand the finality of what you are doing. He will ask you if you realize that you have the first right to parent, and if you understand your right to AFDC (Aid to Families and Dependent Children). He'll also want you to tell him in your own words *why* you feel the best interest of the child is served by placing him in an adoptive home. Before the judge talks with you, the social worker will present all the signed legal papers (called affidavits), which are signed by you several days in advance of the hearing. Once the judge feels confident that you have made a thoughtful and thorough decision, he will approve and sign the affidavit granting the order for termination of parental rights.

Q.Can I, as a birth mother, locate my child?

A.When you terminate parental rights, you are giving up all rights ever to see the child again. However, if you are interested in a reunion, you may contact the agency that helped you place your child and request assistance. You may also ask for non-identifying information about how the child is doing, or ask for direct contact. You must remember, however, that if the child is under nineteen, the adoptive parents can decide whether or not they will provide this information.

Now that we have answered some typical questions about the adoption process, if you have decided to release your child, you will want to know what's in store concerning the emotional aspects of this decision.

What to Expect Following Delivery

After your baby is born, you may feel excited, content with your decision, and glad the pregnancy is over. Or confusion, panic, and uncertainty may set in. It's perfectly natural and typical to have those ups and downs. You may have deep reservations about saying goodby. If this happens, reevaluate your decision and restudy your options.

You need to know that some people won't know how to respond. They may not know what to say. But for your own sense of well-being, encourage those friends who can allow you to talk about your baby to come visit you. Express your grief openly. Don't allow it to build inside, only to come out perhaps years later. The following interview with one young unwed mother shows that it was good for her to verbalize her thoughts to us.

Kristi Reflects

The day after I found out about my pregnancy, I knew my mom had to be told. Here's the shocker: for some reason mom strongly suspected and wasn't all that surprised! Still, it took her a week before we could talk about the problem.

I tried to look at it from her angle, and I knew if our roles were switched, I'd be mad too. I couldn't tell my dad. Mom told him. He didn't say a word. It was something he'd rather not discuss.

As soon as mom knew, she asked me to talk with our pastor. He strongly urged that I find some counseling, and he advised me to take my time in making any decision.

I have good feelings concerning the group meetings I attended at the counseling center. The people there helped to show me what other teens in my situation were going through. The group interaction was important to me. It was interesting to listen to the other young women's reactions to their problem, and hear about how their relatives and friends were treating them. I also made some good friends at the center. I will never forget when one of the young women said, "It's not fair for me to raise the baby all alone while he [the birth father] is still running around." That statement really hit me!

When I pictured myself placing the baby, it was tough. I knew I wouldn't be able to see him or know where he lived. Nor would I have the chance to see his first tooth, or be with him for his first haircut.

One thing that helped was that no one pushed me to make my decision. In the beginning I knew there was a lot of time to make it. But that kind of worked against me, because I procrastinated and kept putting it off.

The way I finally made my choice for adoption was to contemplate the pros and cons. If I kept, then I'd need to quit both school and my job, because mom worked full-time. I wouldn't have money to live elsewhere, and I would most likely end up on AFDC. When I wrote the pros and cons on a piece of paper, it was obvious what I should do.

A few people's reactions were negative. The one question that came up most was "How could you give away your baby?" They tried to make me feel guilty, like I was copping out. But when people asked me, I just explained I couldn't afford to raise a child, that I'm not the *only* one responsible for him, and that I felt a one-parent home wouldn't be fair to the baby.

After a while, kids at school said they respected me for my decision. The funny thing, though, was that they didn't come right out and tell me. I had to hear it through the grapevine. I wish they'd have come to me and offered some support. However, my teachers told me face to face they thought I did the right thing. Of course my parents were relieved. They wanted me to place and felt it was best all along.

This experience has matured me. I can make decisions better because now I look at all the angles, then decide. My parents and I have grown closer. We communicate more, talk openly about things now, and they support me with love.

I have a few suggestions for any young woman who is going to place her child: Try to get back to work or school as soon as possible. Also, recognize that people *will* question you about it. They will still wonder, and some may even be critical of you. Don't take their comments too seriously. No one can tell you if it was the right decision or not. *You* are the only person capable of that.

If *your* choice, like Kristi's, is to place your child for adoption, what about your feelings?

What Happens Now?

How you cope with loss is up to you. It is advisable not to dwell on negatives. Instead, remind yourself of all the positive reasons for this choice. When you pray, ask God to bless the child and be with him and his new family. Lastly, focus your thoughts on the beautiful gift you gave your child—the gift of life.

Of course, it took a "significant other" to help you begin that life. Next you will want to see how your boyfriend fits into the crisis pregnancy picture.

12.
What About Him?

This book has focused mainly on you and your baby to this point. But you will also want to examine what involvement the birth father will have. Is he willing to support you with love? Or does he act as if he's never met you before?

It's great if your boyfriend is willing to be involved with the pregnancy, because you need a lot of emotional support at this time. However, as Beth is discovering, this can be carried too far.

Beth is an attractive nineteen-year-old who knows there is no future in her relationship with Todd, aged sixteen. She realizes Todd is childish, bossy, and too young for her, but she can't bring herself to break up with him yet.

"I will allow him to be in the labor and delivery room with me," Beth explained, "then tell him it's all over between us." Beth wouldn't listen to her counselor, who warned that the birth experience will become an intimate bonding between parents and child. This will make it ten times more difficult to say goodby to Todd.

Our best advice to young women in a crisis pregnancy is this: If his choice is to stick by you, but you don't definitely plan to marry him, remain strong and only let him be involved as much or little as *you* want.

Don't leave him out entirely, but don't allow him to run your life either.

Some pregnancy centers have groups specifically designed to support birth fathers. Early on, if he's willing to go, encourage him toward this kind of counseling.

Then again, sometimes young women just can't predict how their "significant other" will take the idea of suddenly being thrust into the role of a father.

Some Typical Reactions of Birth Fathers

BRAD

At age eighteen, Brad was excited at the prospect of being a father. He was also demanding. His attitude toward Lori was, "I have my rights too, and I will be in that labor room with you." He has possessive tendencies, but is the dependent one in the relationship. Although he just graduated from high school, he is still quite irresponsible. Nevertheless, he's told Lori she must keep the baby and marry him.

TIM

Here is a young man who's an expert at avoiding the issue. Since he found out that Patti is pregnant, he's had no contact whatsoever with her. Patti, after delivering their child, can't understand why the baby's father doesn't even want to see him. The simple reason is that Tim is running scared.

BRIAN

Brian is cautious. He wants to provide emotional support, but not too much. "I'm afraid I'll be pinned down with the responsibility of a wife and family. If that happens, my goal of becoming an airline pilot will be shot. I guess my preference is for her to give the baby up. If she keeps it, how will I ever pay the child support?"

JOHNNY

At fifteen, John has a predictably immature reaction. "I don't give a rip what Charla does with the kid. It's not mine anyway. What do I care?" Johnny really doesn't know how to react, so he puts up defenses. Though he is hurting inside, he appears to be cool and crass.

Cornelius Tacitus, a historian born in A.D. 55, once said, "It is part of human nature to hate the person you have hurt." Johnny's reaction certainly supports this statement. But it's also true that as humans, we tend to hate those who have hurt us.

Your reaction to the birth father could be anger or bitterness. Or you might feel guilty because you ended your relationship with him when you found out you were pregnant, and he wanted you to remain his friend and keep the child. Are you suffering hurt and rejection because you depended on him and now he has dumped you? This reaction usually brings on the depressing feeling of being used. However, no matter how he has treated you, there are still legal aspects he needs to face.

What Are His Legal Responsibilities?

The book *Mom . . . I'm Pregnant* by Bev O'Brien says it best.

> Our lawyer advised us that if Sandy had a good case against Jim, he would be legally responsible for all of the expenses directly associated with Sandy's pregnancy, as well as for child support (should Sandy decide to raise her baby herself) until the child reached the age of eighteen. . . .
>
> After assessing the facts, our lawyer felt that Sandy did have a good case, and he recommended sending a Letter of Demand to Jim. In it, Jim was requested to pay for those expenses Sandy had listed. The letter also notified Jim that he would be subject to payment of further pregnancy-related expenses, and possibly child support payments.
>
> When Jim failed to respond to this action, our lawyer discussed further steps he could take.
>
> "I can either file a claim in court on Sandy's behalf, or I can file a paternity suit against the baby's alleged father . . . ."
>
> He explained what was involved. If necessary the judge may order medical testing (which is much improved in its reliability in recent years) to establish paternity.
>
> The judge will listen to testimony for both the baby's mother and alleged father. If, in the judge's opinion, there is reason to believe that the alleged father is the father indeed, then the paternity of the baby is established. The father is then required to pay court costs, and to pay whatever expenses and child support that the judge decrees.[1]

What Are His Legal Rights?

You need to be aware that once paternity has been established, and he is ordered to reimburse your

[1]Bev O'Brien, *Mom . . . I'm Pregnant* (Wheaton, Ill.: Tyndale House, 1982), 85–87.

expenses, the father may also stake a claim on the baby. Out of stubbornness, resentment, misguided bravery or whatever, either he may refuse to give his permission to place the baby for adoption, or he may seek visitation rights or even permanent custody of the child.

What's in Store?

No matter what your feelings toward each other are, try to look at this time as a period of growth for both of you. Your relationship can take one of two paths. This crisis will either draw you closer or drive you apart.

QUESTIONS TO CONSIDER:

1. Would you want the relationship to be different in any way?
2. How could you improve it?
3. Has your relationship changed during pregnancy? How?
4. What kind of relationship would you like the baby to have with his father?
5. If you keep the baby and choose not to marry, what would you want the baby to know about his father?
6. What kind of feelings do you have toward your boyfriend's parents?
7. What interest do you wish them to have in the baby?

What About Your Own Parents?

As we stated earlier, your pregnancy has had a profound effect on your parents' lives also. For some parents, the shock of a daughter becoming a mother is bound to erupt in a display of emotional fireworks. They may explode at first, then slowly come to accept the situation. For others, the news that they are soon to be grandparents will come as a not-so-pleasant surprise, but still something they can handle. Or your parents may fit into an entirely different category.

To prepare you for a typical reaction, read on to see how some parents feel about their daughter's "delicate condition."

13.
Grandparents Have Feelings Too
An Open Letter to Parents

Dear Parents,

Dealing with the pressure-cooker emotions that swell with the discovery of a pregnant daughter, I seesawed from denying it was true, to accepting, to hoping for a miscarriage, to loving her, to wanting her to go somewhere, have the baby and pretend it never happened. On top of everything else, if she chose to complete the pregnancy, this would be our first grandchild. I'm too young to say I had actually dreamed of this day, but the thought had momentarily flitted through my mind.

Kind and dear friends told me it happens all the time. *Not to my girl*, I silently screamed. She had played the Virgin Mary in a play during high school—and fit the part. How could this happen?

My and myself, went to a Crisis Pregnancy Center for help. We needed a "third person" to help us talk and work through our feelings. We agreed on one thing. We loved each other. This was not going to break up our family. Somehow, whatever our daughter decided, we were going to stick together. Even friends do that. My suggestion to you as parents, is to remain a friend to your daughter too. No matter what.

Written by one who's been there.

Reactions of Expectant Grandparents

No two people except siblings have the same set of parents. For this reason, if you have a friend who's experienced a crisis pregnancy, your mom and dad probably won't react the way her parents did. Here are examples of how some parents took the news. You may or may not see your mom and dad among them.

SARAH

Believe it or not, Sarah's parents were excited when she told them she was pregnant. They both loved babies and were already stand-in grandparents to the neighborhood children. There was no doubt in their minds that they would want to adopt their own flesh and blood. "We felt we'd been given a second chance at parenting a baby from early infancy, and we anxiously awaited our grandchild's birth," they explained. "Of course we were unhappy at first that Sarah chose to loosen the reins on her morals, but we know she's sorry for it and that's what's important."

PAM

Pam's mom and dad took a different attitude. They wanted her to abort, but she was too far along in the pregnancy. Their next choice was to hide her in a foster home seventy-five miles away. "I don't know that I can ever forgive her for the shame she's caused us," her mom admitted. "Her dad and I are going for counseling now to try to work through the bitterness."

TINA

Tina's folks absolutely refused to discuss the pregnancy with her. They were trapped in the denial stage. When faced with the actual birth, they felt that Tina had no choice but to place it. "I'm sorry to have this attitude, but I can't help it," her dad said. "I don't want Tina's kid around to remind me of my failure as a father."

AMY

By contrast, Amy's parents became very close to her through Amy's pregnancy. Her mother, who had had to get married herself, was extremely supportive and sympathetic. She didn't try to influence Amy one way or another, but instead allowed her to make her own decision. "How could I help but love my daughter through this? We all make mistakes," her mother said. "Not one of us is perfect. What possible good would it do to be angry with her?"

Negative Attitudes Can Change

No matter how your parents first reacted to the crisis pregnancy, their thoughts and feelings may change over the next nine-to-twelve months. In a touching personal experience book, *Mom . . . I'm Pregnant* Bev O'Brien relates how, after a disagreement with her nineteen-year-old daughter, the daughter leaves and doesn't come home for several hours. While worrying over her child's emotional and physical well-being, Mrs. O'Brien explains how she steps onto the road marked "Acceptance."

"During those anxious hours, I discovered the key to

my acceptance of Sandy's pregnancy. I had to stop thinking of myself, and to begin thinking of Sandy.

"I had to face that deep chasm which separated my initial reaction from my ultimate acceptance, walk right up to the edge, and make the leap. The longer I hesitated, peering down at all those monsters—guilt, fear of the unknown, unwillingness to look truth in the eye, self-pity—the harder it would be to make myself jump."[1]

Many parents, upon first learning of their daughter's pregnancy, will react with anger, hurt, and guilt. In a poignant excerpt from *What's the Matter With Christy?* Ruth Allen, a mother of six and a pastor's wife, shares her tender feelings concerning her youngest daughter's pregnancy:

Oh God! There is so much pain inside me.

I am no stranger to trouble—it seems as though I never have been. There's always been physical and mental suffering of some kind for me. But now life is upside down, and it seems as though it will never be right side up.

This is such a bitter disappointment, Lord! Christy's just fifteen; she's just a baby! My precious little girl—pregnant! I don't know what we're going to do.

Right now I can think of so many things we might have done differently. We should never have let her go out on that first date with him. Why didn't we insist? Because we didn't want to fight with her. What a price to pay for keeping the peace!

Why Lord? Why does my heart ache so? I wonder about me. Is it because of me that some of our children have chosen to walk on paths of rebellion and pain? That one nightmare follows another?

[1]Bev O'Brien, *"Mom . . . I'm Pregnant"* (Wheaton, Ill.: Tyndale House, 1982), 19.

This pain is too much to bear. I don't know how I can live through another day. Oh, Lord, where *are* You in the midst of my misery and tears?

But, I remember that in the past there were darker days than this one. Through physical and mental illness, through emotional torment, you calmed me and gave me peace and strength that I never knew existed. You have brought me through many stormy seas and troubled waters.

I look to You now, Lord. Help me! Help us![2]

Your Goal

Your goal for your parents should be for them to face your pregnancy honestly. No matter what their initial reaction is, realize it doesn't necessarily change the love they have for you.

Your mother and father may need counseling to help them deal with their feelings. "Time heals all wounds" is a good phrase to remember. If they are agreeable, urge them toward meeting with your social worker so they too can gain further support.

Put Yourself in Their Shoes

Consider your parents' perception of out-of-wedlock pregnancy. Back when they grew up, it was something criticized. The unwed mother was almost always sent away. She was judged to be *a bad girl* or *fallen woman*. Thirty years ago, unless there was a hastily arranged wedding, it was almost unheard of to keep the child. Our society is more accepting, and there are many resources to call on for help.

[2]Ruth Allen, *What's the Matter With Christy?* (Minneapolis, Minn.: Bethany House Publishers, 1982), 15–16.

The Case for Positive Counseling

We have stressed in previous chapters how important it is for you to seek professional help; but it is also advisable that your parents get counseling. There are many excellent reasons why they should talk with an objective professional. A trained counselor can help to resolve negative feelings like guilt, anger, denial, and frustration. She can also help them to be honest with you in terms of what you can and cannot expect from them.

Most parents are too close to the problem to be objective. Counseling can provide your mother and father with the tools to "back off" and allow you to come to your own decision. A trained professional could steer them toward letting go of some of the responsibility. She could assist your parents toward being alert to your needs, yet also help establish the fact that they are not responsible for the choice you make concerning the baby.

It may be hard for your parents to cope with their daughter's growing up so fast and her taking on adult obligations quickly. If your mom has protected and sheltered you all your life, it's going to be pretty hard for her to suddenly take off on a shopping trip with you to buy maternity clothes. But counseling can help her and your father work through the upset, confused feelings they may experience.

Potential for Growing Closer

Your crisis pregnancy may be an event that draws your family into a closer relationship. Before their daughter's pregnancy, some parents appear too busy to care. Then an amazing thing happens. In many cases, the family of a pregnant young woman binds tightly together and provides her with emotional support. Suddenly all their efforts are devoted toward uplifting their daughter with positive reinforcement. We hope this holds true for you and that you will be able to observe your parents' real concern and their desire to offer helpful, loving support.

Some mothers are skillful in talking with their daughters about the changes that occur during pregnancy. This discussion in itself forms a special bonding that wasn't there before. It then becomes more natural to delve further into sharing inner thoughts and feelings between mother and daughter.

Your months of pregnancy can also be useful as a time of evaluating future goals. Intimacy guidelines may be reestablished. Priorities, when thoroughly discussed with your family, may shed new light on what issues are really important in your life.

A View From the Other Side

In chapter 11 you read about Kristi. Let's see how her mother coped with Kris's problem.

I think going through Kris's older sister's pregnancy helped me face Kris's problem. When she got pregnant, I got as much help for her as I could. I knew from past experience that I just had to get professional support for her.

There are lots of benefits gained from counseling. It's been well worth the time and expense involved. I'm so thankful our pastor directed us toward a crisis pregnancy center.

As soon as parents are aware of their daughter's pregnancy, they need to get started with counseling right away.

Whether your parents offer loving support or are totally furious over your condition, one fact remains; there *is* Someone who will stand by you and see you through the crisis pregnancy. And ever after too. If you don't already know Him, the last chapter can help you make His acquaintance.

14.
Faith Helps

Like most single and pregnant young women, you probably wonder, *Why, of all people, did this have to happen to me?* Three quotations from the book *Apples Of Gold* may specifically apply to your situation.

The diamond cannot be polished without friction, nor man perfected without trials.

God never makes us conscious of our weakness except to give us of His strength.

The difference between stumbling blocks and stepping stones is the way a man uses them.[1]

Stumbling Block or Stepping Stone

Your choice to give another human being a chance at life is in keeping with God's plan. You might believe your pregnancy is a stumbling block. But God desires to turn your experience into a stepping stone toward Him.

Did you know that Psalm 139 applies to *both* you and your baby?

[1]Jo Petty, ed., *Apples of Gold* (Norwalk, Conn.: C. R. Gibson Co., 1962), 44, 46.

"For you created my inmost being; you knit me together in my mother's womb. I praise you because I am fearfully and wonderfully made; your works are wonderful, I know that full well. My frame was not hidden from you when I was made in the secret place. When I was woven together in the depths of the earth, your eyes saw my unformed body. All the days ordained for me were written in your book before one of them came to be" (Psalm 139:13–16).

Did you discover the significant words? *He saw us before we were ever born?* Mind-boggling, isn't it? God is keenly aware of our situation. He isn't just standing around watching it happen!

Many times we can't understand why certain things take place in our lives. We call them stumbling blocks. Cringing in the middle of the cyclone, we wonder if God's on vacation. But God needs no rest, even from all our doubts. He promises He will be right in the cyclone with us. "And surely I am with you always, to the very end of the age" (Matthew 28:20). From the moment you chosrry your baby full-term, God chose to bless you because of your refusal to tamper with someone else's life.

However, it's unrealistic to think there won't be any pain, sorrow, or difficulty involved. It is best to look at the situation as a learning experience, a step toward faith, maturity, and emerging as a better person.

"Growth Spurts"

Here are some excerpts from interviews with pregnant singles who have discovered blessings out of seeming brokenness:

ANNE

"I never used to be close to my parents until I became pregnant. Then everything changed. For the first time, I felt their love and support toward me. But on the other hand, maybe I just opened my eyes and saw them for who they really are—parents who *always* cared. Seeing me in trouble was the key for them to openly express their affection. And for me to receive it."

SHELLEY

"Before I got pregnant I was only concerned about wearing the latest fashions and getting time off work to go out with my friends. My crisis pregnancy forced me to grow up, make some mature decisions and figure out what to do with my future."

RITA

"Going through this pregnancy was the most difficult thing I ever did. But I wouldn't have it any other way because, not only have I experienced the miracle of life, but through reading the Bible, I also met the Creator of Life and His Son, whom I've come to accept and love. As I look back, I *know* it was the love of Jesus that carried me through the last year."

He Will Carry You Too

You are never going to be the same person you were before pregnancy. God knows those changes can be scary, and He wants you to know He will travel the road right along with you. His Word, the Bible, promises this: "Yet I am always with you; you hold me by my right hand. You guide me with your counsel. . ." (Psalm 73:23–24).

If you are God's daughter, the words "But even so" cover any sins, sexual or otherwise, you may commit. When you are under His authority, God still loves you, no matter what you do.

God states in Psalm 32:8, "I will instruct you and teach you in the way you should go; I will counsel you and watch over you." This means He will watch over, care for, and love you through the progression of your pregnancy, and ever afterward. You can believe it. He is a God of truth.

Here is another comforting promise, "So do not fear, for I am with you; do not be dismayed, for I am your God. I will strengthen you and help you; I will uphold you with my righteous right hand" (Isaiah 41:10). Webster's Dictionary says "uphold" means to support, advocate, and confirm. God wants you to know that *He* is your biggest supporter.

Grab Hold of Him!

If you would like to be on God's team, but don't know how to make Him captain of your life, it's easy. Believe that He sent His Son Jesus to pay for your sins once and for all on Calvary's cross. Read His Word. It's God's love letter to the world, and all the magnificent promises within are written to *you*.

Becoming a Christian is so simple that many people fall over the concept. They think that being a good person or doing nice things will get them into heaven. Not necessarily. The way to grab hold of Him is to confess your sins (*all* of us are sinners), then believe and accept God's perfect gift.

"Jesus answered, 'I am the way and the truth and the life. No one comes to the Father except through me'" (John 14:6). As you believe and receive, you assure yourself of a permanent home in heaven. The problems you face now and the life you live on earth are temporary. Eternity is forever. You can, if you choose, spend it with God.

SUGGESTED PRAYER:

> Dear Lord,
> As I make these decisions, please be
> *before* me to show me the right way,
> *behind* me for encouragement,
> *beside* me for friendship,
> *above* me for protection, and
> *within*, to give me your peace.
> Amen.

Bibliography

Allen, Ruth. *"What's the Matter with Christy?"* Minneapolis, Minn.: Bethany House Publishers, 1982.

Burgess, Linda Cannon. *The Art of Adoption.* New York: W. W. Norton & Co., 1981.

Business Week. April 22, 1985, 58–59.

Clinebell, Howard J., Jr. *Basic Types of Pastoral Counseling,* rev. ed. Nashville: Abingdon Press, 1966.

Critelli, Ida, and Tom Schick. *Unmarried and Pregnant: What Now?* Cincinnati: St. Anthony Messenger Press, 1977.

FDA Consumer. June, 1989. 9–10.

"Health Tips." A publication of the California Medical and Research Foundation. Index WH–45. March 1989.

Johnson, R. Janet, and Diane Pankow. *Pre-natal Care, Loving Before Birth.* Weymouth, Mass.: Life Skills Education, 1989.

Klein, Carole. *The Single Parent Experience.* New York: Avon Books, 1973.

The Living Bible, paraphrased. Wheaton, Ill.: Tyndale House Publishers, 1971.

March of Dimes Foundation Alert Bulletin 29. White Plains, N.Y.: National Foundation Headquarters. (This bulletin is no longer published.)

Markell, Jan, and Jane Winn. *Overcoming Stress.* Wheaton, Ill.: Victor Books, 1982.

Morrison, Margaret. "When Your Baby's Life Is So Much Your Own," *FDA Consumer* 13 (May 1979).

O'Brien, Bev. *"I'm Pregnant."* Wheaton, Ill.: Tyndale House Publishers, 1982.

Petty, Jo, compiler. *Apples of Gold.* Norwalk, Conn.: C. R. Gibson Co., 1962.

Tanner, Ira J. *Healing the Pain of Everyday Loss.* Minneapolis: Winston Press, 1980.

Walling, Regis. *When Pregnancy Is a Problem.* St. Meinrad, Ind.: Abbey Press, 1980.

Suggestions for Further Reading

Allen, Ruth. *"What's Happened to Christy?"* Bethany House Publishers, 1982.

Ashley, Meg. *Meg: A True Story.* Living Books, Tyndale House Publishers, 1980.

Bel Geddes, Joan. *How to Parent Alone: A Guide For Single Parents.* Seabury Press, 1974.

DiGiulio, Robert. *When You Are A Single Parent.* St. Meinrad: Abbey Press, 1979.

Dobson, James. *Dare To Discipline.* Tyndale House Publishers, 1970.

Dobson, James. *Parenting Isn't for Cowards.* Word Books, 1988.

Johnson, Lisa Halls. *Just Like Ice Cream.* Ronald N. Haynes Publishers, 1982.

Klein, Carole. *The Single Parent Experience.* Avon Books, 1978.

Lindsay, Jeanne Warren. *Pregnant Too Soon: Adoption Is an Option.* EMC Publishing, 1980.

Narramore, Bruce. *Help! I'm A Parent* (with manual *A Guide to Child Rearing*). Zondervan Publishing House, 1972.

O'Brien, Bev. *"Mom . . . I'm Pregnant."* Tyndale House Publishers, 1982.

Shaffer, Betty. *Lisa*. Bethany House Publishers, 1982.

Walling, Regis. *When Pregnancy Is a Problem*. Abbey Press, 1980.

Watts (Smith), Virginia. *The Single Parent*. Fleming H. Revell, 1976, rev. ed. 1983.

Crisis Pregnancy Centers

(Arranged alphabetically by states)

Alaska

Anchorage Crisis Preg. Center
3020 Minnesota Drive, STE 9
Anchorage, AK 99503
907-276-4767

TLC Preg. Testing & Counseling
600 3rd St. - Graehl
Fairbanks, AK 99701
907-456-3719

Homer CPC
P.O. Box 2
Homer, AK 99603
907-235-7899

Kodiak CPC
P.O. Box 3568
Kodiak, AK 99615
907-486-8418

Valley CPC
951 East Bogard, Suite 103
Wasilla, AK 99687
907-373-3456

Arizona

CPC of Apache Junction
447 E. Broadway, Suite 3
Apache Junction, AZ 85220
602-966-5683

CPC W. Phoenix
5955 W. Myrtle, Suite 3
Glendale, AZ 85301
602-254-4999

CPC's of Greater Phoenix
301 W. Osborn, Suite B 114
Phoenix, AZ 85103
602-274-1770

We Care CPC
1989 South Frontage Rd., #A
Sierra Vista, AZ 85635
602-459-5683

The CPC
960 W. University Suite 102
Tempe, AZ 85281
602-829-0398

The CPC
1124 North Third Avenue
Tucson, AZ 85705
602-622-5774

California

Tree Of Life CPC
5970 Entrada #B
Atascadero, CA 93422

Bakersfield CPC
2920 F Street, Suite C-5
Bakersfield, CA 93301
805-326-1907

Berkeley CPC
2991 Shattuck Ave., Suite 201
Berkeley, CA 94705
415-849-9916

The Pregnancy Center
5047 Clayton Road
Concord, CA 94521
415-827-0100

New Life CPC
P.O. Box 861
Crescent City, CA 95531
707-464-3233

Davis CPC
328 D Street
Davis, CA 95617
916-753-0110

San Diego Pregnancy Services
1083 Broadway, Suite F
El Cajon, CA 92021
619-440-0834

Pregnant and Single

Central Valley CPC
1304 East Olive
Fresno, CA 93728
209-485-5444

Pregnancy Help Center Glendale
144 S. Maryland, Suite 204
Glendale, CA 91205
818-247-6554

Nevada Co. CPC
113 Presley Way, Ste 4
Grass Valley, CA 95945
916-272-6800

Kings County CPC
206 W. Lacey Blvd A
Hanford, CA 93230
209-583-1900

Crisis Pregnancy Services
910 Monterey Street, #10
Hollister, CA 95023
408-637-4020

A Woman's Friend CPC
616 E Street #A
Marysville, CA 95901
916-741-9136

Alpha House CPC
P.O. Box 3168
Merced, CA 95344
209-383-4700

Santa Clara Co. CPC
2425 California Street
Mountain View, CA 94040
415-964-8093

Pregnancy Res. Ctr. of Marin
7075 Redwood Blvd., Suite E
Novato, CA 94945
415-892-0558

San Diego Pregnancy Services
2191 El Camino Real # 201
Oceanside, CA 92054
619-722-7358

Living Well Clinic
293 South Main Street
Orange, CA 92668
714-633-4673

CPC of Monterey Peninsula
1117 Forest Avenue
Pacific Grove, CA 93950
408-373-8535

Valley CPC
7660 Amador Valley Blvd.
Pleasanton, CA 94568
415-828-4458

Plumas CPC
P.O. Box 1800
Quincy, CA 95971
916-283-1002

CPC of Northern California
2525 Victor Avenue, Suite B
Redding, CA 96002
916-221-0337

CPC of Sacramento
2222 Watt Avenue, #D6
Sacramento, CA 95825
916-972-0299

CPC of Salinas
P.O. Box 4915
Salinas, CA 93901
408-757-5510

CPC of San Francisco
1350-A Lawton Street
San Francisco, CA 94122
415-753-8000

CPC of Santa Clara
1150 Hilldale Ave., Suite 104
San Jose, CA 95118
408-978-9310

San Mateo County CPC
318 South B Street
San Mateo, CA 94401
405-340-1232

SCV Pregnancy Center
24303 Walnut Street Suite F
Santa Clarita, CA 91321
805-255-0084

CPC of Santa Cruz Inc.
911 Center St.
Santa Cruz, CA 95060
408-458-3335

Pregnancy Counseling Center
1100 Sonoma Ave., Suite E
Santa Rosa, CA 95405
707-575-3429

CPC of So. Lake Tahoe
PO Box 13351
South Lake Tahoe, CA 95702
916-577-5433

Conejo Valley CPC, Suite 11
1421 E. Thousand Oaks
Thousand Oaks, CA 91362
805-373-1222

CPC of Tracy
PO Box 1237
Tracy, CA 95376-1237
209-836-4415

Pregnancy Counseling Center
331 N. School Street
Ukiah, CA 95482
707-463-1436

East Bag CPC
4 Union Square #B
Union City, CA 94587
415-487-4357

Ventura County CPC
3212 Loma Vista Rd., Suite 220
Ventura, CA 93003
805-656-1005

CPC of Tulare County
208 W. Main Suite M
Visalia, CA 93291
209-625-5550

Colorado

Valley CPC
PO Box 10207
Aspen, CO 81612
303-920-3737

Boulder CPC
999 Alpine
Boulder, CO 80302
303-494-3262

Abundant Life CPC
PO Box 2002
Canon City, CO 81215-2002
719-275-7074

Colorado Springs Pregnancy Ctr
3700 Galley Road
Colorado Springs, CO 80909
719-591-2724

Yampa Valley CPC
312 W. Victory Way
Craig, CO 81625
303-824-5204

Pregnancy Resource Center
P.O. Box 165
Delta, CO 81416
303-874-5733

The Pregnancy Center *
1005 N 12th St. Suite 103
Grand Junction, CO 81501
303-241-7474

CPC of Northern County
1020 9th Street, #305
Greeley, CO 80631
303-353-2673

Pregnancy Assistance League
P.O. Box 462
Lamar, CO 81052
719-336-7568

Longmont CPC
16 Mountain View Avenue #115
Longmont, CO 80501
303-651-2050

CPC of Montrose
P.O. Box 563
Montrose, CO 81402
303-249-4302

Women's Pregnancy Center
106 W 2nd St.
Pueblo, CO 81003
719-544-9312

Colorado Springs Pregnancy Ctr
P.O. Box 5166
Woodland Park, CO 80866
719-591-2724

Connecticut

Caring Family Pregnancy Serv.
P.O. Box 752
Danielson, CT 06239
203-779-0218

Pregnant and Single

CPC
30 Mill St.
Unionville, CT 06085
203-673-7397

Delaware

Problem Pregnancy Center Inc.
235 W. Lockerman St.
Dover, DE 19901
302-734-2233

Sussex County CPC
P.O. Box 23
Georgetown, DE 19947
302-856-4344

New Castle County CPC
325 E. Main Street, Suite 303
Newark, DE 19711
302-366-0285

New Castle CPC
911 Washington Street
Wilmington, DE 19801
302-575-0309

Florida

TLC Women's Pregnancy Center
119 W. Palmetto Park Road
Boca Raton, FL 33432
407-392-3446

A Woman's Pregnancy Center
1324 E. Commercial Blvd.
Fort Lauderdale, FL 33334
305-491-2766

CPC of Gainesville
1441 NW 6th Street
Gainesville, FL 32601
904-377-4947

A Woman's Pregnancy Center
40 Southeast 4th Road
Homestead, FL 33030
305-245-4673

Pregnancy Crisis Center
217 So. Columbia Street
Lake City, FL 32055
904-755-0058

Pregnancy Resources, Inc.
110 Bry Lynn Drive
Melbourne, FL 32904
305-768-1340

A Woman's Pregnancy Center
7575 S.W. 62nd Ave.
Miami, FL 33143
305-665-4673

Bay County CPC
PO Box 937
Panama City, FL 32402
904-763-1100

Pregnancy Ctr of Pinellas Cty
9745 66th Street, North
Pinellas Park, FL 34666
813-545-1234

A Women's Pregnancy Center
1225 Miccosukee Rd.
Tallahassee, FL 32303
904-877-4774

Vero Beach CPC
P.O. Box 836
Vero Beach, FL 32960
305-569-7939

Alpha Care Pregnancy Center
2215 N. Military Trail, A-1
West Palm Beach, FL 33417
407-478-2644

Georgia

Greater Augusta CPC
P.O. Box 1755
Augusta, GA 30903
404-724-5531

Crisis Pregnancy Center
2080 Fairburn Rd., Suite A-2
Douglasville, GA 30135
404-920-1001

La Grange CPC
PO Box 2201
La Grange, GA 30241
404-884-3833

Iowa

Life CPC
P.O. Box 961
Clinton, IA 52732
319-242-6628

Forest City CPC
131 N. Clark Street
Forest City, IA 50436
515-582-5419

Home & Family Care
P.O. Box 3413
Iowa City, IA 52244
319-351-6556

Mason City CPC
1631 Fourth St., S.W.
Mason City, IA 50401
515-357-8220

Idaho

Open Door Pregnancy Center
312 South Washington, #3
Moscow, ID 83843
208-882-2370

Lifeline CPC
1323 12th Avenue, South
Nampa, ID 83651
208-466-4000

Illinois

Eastern Illinois Save-A-Baby
P.O. Box 271
Charleston, IL 61920

Loop CPC
104 S. Michigan #727
Chicago, IL 60603
312-263-1576

Uptown CPC
939 W. Wilson
Chicago, IL 60640
312-989-2095

Southside CPC
3208 W. 59th St.
Chicago, IL 60629
312-476-6242

Northside CPC
3425 W. Peterson
Chicago, IL 60659
312-463-5930

New Life Pregnancy Center
240 West Main Street
Decatur, IL 62523-2604
217-429-0464

CPC of the Fox Valley
309 Ryerson
Elgin, IL 60123
708-697-0203

Metro East CPC
2122 E. Pontoon Road
Granite City, IL 62040
618-451-2002

CP Services of DuPage County
890 E. Roosevelt Road
Lombard, IL 60148
708-495-9101

Northside CPC
1535 Lake Cook Road, #501
Northbrook, IL 60062
708-291-9966

Women's Pregnancy Center
P.O. Box 822
Peoria, IL 61652
309-688-0202

CPC of Livingston Co
P.O. Box 417
Pontiac, IL 61764
815-842-2484

Northern Illinois CPC
1509 E. State St.
Rockford, IL 61108
815-398-5444

Twin City CPC
P.O. Box 286
Sterling, IL 61081
815-625-5300

Pregnancy Aid South Suburbs
6744 West 173rd Street
Tinley Park, IL 60477
708-614-9777

131

Pregnant and Single

Tri-County CPC
P.O. Box 322
Wauconda, IL 60084
708-526-0960

Indiana

Alpha CPC
24 W. 17th Street
Anderson, IN 46016
317-649-0449

Central Indiana CPC (East)
PO Box 19870
Indianapolis, IN 46219
317-359-1600

Central Indiana CPC (West)
P.O. Box 22175
Indianapolis, IN 46222
317-923-1199

Central Indiana CPC - Admin.
2105 N. Meridian, Suite 104
Indianapolis, IN 46202
317-925-5437

Heart to Heart CPC Inc.
2204 W. McGalliard Rd.
Muncie, IN 47304
317-286-6060

New Beginnings, Inc CPC
P.O. Box 313
Spencer, IN 47460
812-829-6381

CPC of the Wabash Valley
P.O. Box 3447
Terre Haute, IN 47803
812-234-8059

RAPP CPC
702 Browne St.
Winchester, IN 47394
317-584-2442

Kansas

Midwest CPC
106 E. Chestnut
Independence, KS 67301
316-331-0700

Pregnancy Crisis Center
040 N. West St.
Wichita, KS 67203
316-945-9400

Kentucky

Pregnancy Support Center
P.O. Box 9953
Bowling Green, KY 42101
502-781-5050

Shelter of Love CPC
P.O. Box 393
Morganfield, KY 42437
502-389-2847

Life House CPC
1506 Chestnut Street
Murray, KY 42071
502-753-0700

Hardin Co. CPC
P.O. Box 325
Radcliff, KY 40160
502-352-0717

Louisiana

Crisis Pregnancy Center
4910 Monticello Blvd., Suite B
Baton Rouge, LA 70814
504-272-3680

Northlake CPC
P.O. Box 3198
Covington, LA 70434
504-893-4281

Pregnancy Help Center
727 Robert Blvd.
Slidell, LA 70458
504-643-4357

Massachusetts

Daybreak
1384 Mass Ave
Cambridge, MA 02138
617-576-1981

Precious Life CPC
6 Cherry St.
Haverhill, MA 01830
508-374-0801

Maryland

Greater Baltimore CPC
12 E. 21st St.
Baltimore, MD 21218
301-625-0102

Bowie CPC
4375 Northview
Bowie, MD 20716
301-262-1330

Frederick County CPC
335 E. Church Street
Frederick, MD 21701
301-473-5210

Laurel CPC
415 Main St.
Laurel, MD 20707
301-776-9996

Alpha Pregnancy Center
P.O. Box 495
Reisterstown, MD 21136
301-833-7864

Rockville Pregnancy Center
170 Rollins Avenue, Suite 101
Rockville, MD 20852
301-770-4444

Catherine Foundation CPC
Rt 2 Box 3A
White Plains, MD 20695
301-870-2423

Maine

CPC of Aroostook County
457 Main Street
Presque Isle, ME 04769
207-764-0022

Michigan

CPC Pregnancy Counseling & Ser
153 N. Main Street
Adrian, MI 49221
517-263-5701

Crisis Pregnancy Info. Center
3231 Woodward Avenue
Berkley, MI 48072
313-443-2551

Pregnancy Resource Center
415 Cherry St. SE
Grand Rapids, MI 49503
616-456-6873

Alpha Women's Center
423 Michigan NE
Grand Rapids, MI 49503
616-459-9955

Crisis Pregnancy Services
P.O. Box 1804
Midland, MI 48640
517-835-1500

Central Michigan Pregnancy Ser
P.O. Box 2058
Mount Pleasant, MI 48858
517-773-6008

Muskegon Pregnancy Services
P.O. Box 1703
Muskegon, MI 49443
616-726-2677

CPC of Char-Em
231 State St.
Petoskey, MI 49770
616-348-3388

CPC of Rochester
612 West University
Rochester, MI 48063
313-651-0480

CPC Of Chippewa County
409 Ashmun St., Suite 200
Sault Sainte Marie, MI 49783
906-635-0561

Pregnancy Resource Center
P.O. Box 5363
Traverse City, MI 49685
616-929-3488

West Branch CPC
P.O. Box 513
West Branch, MI 48661
517-345-3909

Minnesota

Caring Pregnancy Center
115 W. 1st Street
Fairmont, MN 56031
507-238-2255

133

Pregnant and Single

Rum River CPC
157 S. Central
Milaca, MN 56353
612-983-3771

New Life Family Services
3361 Republic Ave.
Minneapolis, MN 55426

New Life Family Services
9920 Zilla St., #100
Minneapolis, MN 55433
612-755-3035

New Life Family Services
2031 W. Broadway
Minneapolis, MN 55441
612-522-0613

New Life Family Services
814 N. Broadway
Rochester, MN 55904
507-282-3377

St. Cloud CPC
400 E. St. Germain, #205
Saint Cloud, MN 56304
612-253-1962

New Life Family Services
435 Aldine, Suite 201
Saint Paul, MN 55104
612-641-5595

Missouri

Arnold CPC
1444 Jeffco Blvd.
Arnold, MO 63010
314-296-8431

Greater St. Louis CPC, West
510 Baxter, Suite 10 South
Ballwin, MO 63011
314-277-5111

CPC Of St. Charles County
2352 Hwy 94 S Outer Rd
Saint Charles, MO 63303
314-447-6477

Crisis Pregnancy Center
6744 Clayton Road, Suite 310
Saint Louis, MO 63117
314-645-1424

Mississippi

Golden Triangle CPC
P.O. Box 9334
Columbus, MS 39701
601-327-0501

Montana

Glendive CPC
P.O. Box 254
Glendive, MT 59330
406-365-4051

North Carolina

Pregnancy Support Services
P.O. Box 3062
Chapel Hill, NC 27514
919-942-7318

CPC of Cabarrus County
26 Ardsley Avenue N.E.
Concord, NC 28025
704-782-2221

Pregnancy Support Services
922 Broad Street
Durham, NC 27705
919-493-0450

CPC of Gaston County
1349-B East Garrison Blvd.
Gastonia, NC 28054
704-868-4636

Greensboro CPC
715 N. Eugene Street
Greensboro, NC 27401
919-274-4901

Carolina Pregnancy Center
P.O. Box 1964
Greenville, NC 27835
919-757-0003

Hickory CPC
P.O. Box 9423
Hickory, NC 28603
704-322-4272

Carteret CPC
P.O. Box 1214
Morehead City, NC 28557
919-247-4396

Pregnancy Life Care Center
1321 Oberlin Road
Raleigh, NC 27608
919-832-0890

Rocky Mountain CPC
Station Square Mall, Suite 168
Rocky Mount, NC 27804-1431
919-442-3030

CPC of Cleveland County
P.O. Box 522
Shelby, NC 28150
704-487-4357

Salem Pregnancy Support
503 Thurston St.
Winston-Salem, NC 27103-1609
919-760-3680

North Dakota

Pregnancy Help Center
Box 626 - Highway 17E
Park River, ND 58270
701-284-6601

Nebraska

Lincoln CPC
941 'O' Street, Suite B-
Lincoln, NE 68508
402-475-2501

New Hampshire

CPC of the Twin State Valley
55 Pleasant St., Suite #2
Claremont, NH 03743
603-542-9200

Concord CPC
155 Pleasant Street
Concord, NH 03301
603-224-7477

Sure Hope CPC
P.O. Box 771
Hillsboro, NH 03244
603-464-3299

Lakes Region CPC
506 Union Ave
Laconia, NH 03246
603-528-3121

CPC of the Upper Valley
1 Main Street
Lebanon, NH 03784
603-298-7806

Manchester CPC
510 Chestnut Street
Manchester, NH 03101
603-623-1122

Nashua CPC
33 Main St. Ste 202
Nashua, NH 03060
603-883-9355

Pregnancy Resource Center
P.O. Box 452
Peterborough, NH 03458
603-924-8788

New Jersey

Archway CPC
278 Morris Avenue
Elizabeth, NJ 07208
201-353-0604

Pregnancy Care Center
401 Black Horse Pike
Haddon Heights, NJ 08035
609-547-0055

Liberty CPC
297 Griffith Street
Jersey City, NJ 07307
201-656-6120

Middlesex CPC
550 Union Avenue
Middlesex, NJ 08846
201-560-8080

Friendship Pregnancy Center
P.O. Box 1491
Morristown, NJ 07962
201-538-0967

Helping Hand CPC
P.O. Box 873
Newton, NJ 07860
201-579-2272

Alpha CPC
3515 US Rt. 1
Princeton, NJ 08540
609-921-0494

Pregnant and Single

Helping Hand CPC/
Jersey South
75 West Front Street
Red Bank, NJ 07701
201-747-5454

Cornerstone Pregnancy Center/
South Jersey
261 1/2 East Broadway
Salem, NJ 08079
609-935-0300

Open Door CPC
117 Rt. 37, E.
Toms River, NJ 08753
201-240-5540

Pregnancy Center of Warren
137 Belvidere Avenue
Washington, NJ 07882
201-698-3090

New Mexico

Albuquerque CPC
P.O. Box 27458
Albuquerque, NM 87125
505-243-2020

Gallup CPC
120 S. Boardman Avenue
Gallup,NM 87301
505-722-3445

Nevada

CPC of Carson City
P.O. Box 1176
Carson City, NV 89701
702-885-9190

Las Vegas CPC
721 E. Charleston Blvd. Ste. 6
Las Vegas, NV 89104
702-366-1247

Reno-Sparks CPC
223 Marsh Ave.
Reno, NV 89509
702-322-5544

New York

Alpha CPC
33 Front Street, Room 203
Hempstead, NY 11550
516-489-1766

Hope House Pregnancy Center
121 West Court Street
Ithaca, NY 14850
607-273-4673

New Paltz Pregnancy Support
14-B N. Chestnut Street
New Paltz, NY 12561
914-255-8242

New Promise CPC, Inc.
100 Grand Street
Newburgh, NY 12550
914-561-0833

CPC Oneonta
P.O. Box 362
Oneonta, NY 13820
607-433-1730

Alternative CPC
46 Cannon St.
Poughkeepsie, NY 12601
914-471-9284

CPC Inc.
505 Chili Ave.
Rochester, NY 14611

CPC Oneida County
P.O. Box 722
Rome, NY 13440
315-337-0242

CPC of New York Inc.
322 New Dorp Lane
Staten Island, NY 10306
718-667-4357

S.T.O.P., Inc.
P.O. Box 83
Walworth, NY 14568
315-597-2233

Rockland Pregnancy
Counseling Center
15 Virginia Ave., Suite 4
West Nyack, NY 10994
914-353-1875

Pregnancy Counseling Center of
North Chatau
P.O. Box 423
Westfield, NY 14787
716-326-3401

Ohio

Akron Pregnancy Services
105 East Market Street
Akron, OH 44308
216-434-2221

CPC of Logan County
P.O. Box 487
Bellefontaine, OH 43311
513-592-7735

CPC of Cleveland
Berea Commons, Unit 11
Berea, OH 44017
216-243-2520

First Hope CPC
P.O. Box 555
Bowling Green, OH 43402
419-354-4673

Northwest Ohio CPC
118 W. High Street
Bryan, OH 43506
419-636-5691

Crisis Pregnancy Sprt. Center/
Stark City
P.O. Box 8451
Canton, OH 44714
216-493-3020

Cincinnati CPC
210 Wm Howard Taft Road
Cincinnati. OH 45219
513-961-7778

CPC Cincinnati
3091 W. Galbraith Rd. Ste 305
Cincinnati, OH 45239
513-521-3117

Alternaterm Pregnancy Services
1921 Lee Road
Cleveland, OH 44118
216-371-4848

Miami Valley Women's Center
42 East Rahn Rd., Room 210
Dayton, OH 45409
513-434-1789

Delaware County CPC
P.O. Box 382
Delaware, OH 43015
614-363-7777

The Potter's Pregnancy Center
124 West Fifth Street
East Liverpool, OH 43920
216-386-3999

Lorain County CPC
1138 North Abbe Road
Elyria, OH 44035
216-366-9696

Portage County CPC
P.O. Box 3106
Kent, OH 44240
216-673-4847

Madison County Ohio CPC
P.O. Box 403
London, OH 43140
614-952-0443

AAA Crisis Pregnancy Center
1802 Oberlin Avenue
Lorain, OH 44052
216-282-9777

Richland Pregnancy Services
334 Park Avenue, West
Mansfield, OH 44906
419-552-8862

Middletown CPC
2230 Central Ave.
Middletown, OH 45044
513-424-2229

Knox Pregnancy Services
P.O. Box 606
Mount Vernon, OH 43050
614-393-0370

CPC of Oxford
23 E. High, Suite 3
Oxford, OH 45056
513-523-8866

CPC of Springfield
363 S. Burnett
Springfield, OH 45505
513-323-5725

CPC of Clinton County
132 E. Main Street
Wilmington, OH 45177
513-382-2424

Women's Pregnancy Services
2914-B Cleveland Road
Wooster, OH 44691
216-345-5444

CPC of Mahoning County Inc.
3025 Market Street
Youngstown, OH 44507
216-788-1381

Oklahoma

Alternative Pregnancy Center
3301-B West Broadway
Muskogee, OK 74403
918-683-2020

Oregon

CPC
4240 SW Cedar Hills Blvd.
Beaverton, OR 97005
503-643-4503

Coos County CPC
750 Central
Coos Bay, OR 97420
503-267-5204

Corvallis CPC
765 NW Fifth Street, Suite 303
Corvallis, OR 97330
503-757-9645

Eugene Pregnancy Hotline, Inc.
336 East 11th Street
Eugene, OR 97041
503-345-0400

Pregnancy Crisis Support
240 SE 2nd Ste. D Box 1531
Hermiston, OR 97838
503-567-0888

Pregnancy Counseling Info. Ctr.
P.O. Box 945
McMinnville, OR 97128
503-472-9292

Molalla CPC
P.O. Box 129
Molalla, OR 97038
503-829-2673

Intermountain CPC
P.O. Box 400
Ontario, OR 97914
503-889-4272

CPC
P.O. Box 68504
Portland, OR 97268
503-659-3336

CPC
12709 Northeast Halsey, #B
Portland, OR 97230
503-255-7342

Douglas County CPC
1224 NE. Walnut #136
Roseburg, OR 97470
503-496-0422

Columbia Pregnancy
Counseling
P.O. Box 315
Saint Helens, OR 97051
503-397-6047

Salem Pregnancy Center
P.O. Box 5302
Salem, OR 97304
503-364-2543

Sandy Family Services
P.O. Box 106
Sandy, OR 97055
503-668-8101

Willamette CPC
P.O. Box 9
Sweet Home, OR 97386
503-367-2447

Pennsylvania

Lehigh Valley CPC
29 South 8th Street
Allentown, PA 18101
215-821-0943

Amnion CPC
842 Lancaster Avenue
Bryn Mawr, PA 19010
215-525-1558

Capital Area Pregnancy Center
244 S. 17th Street
Camp Hill, PA 17011
717-761-4411

Pregnancy Ministries
221 Lincoln Way East
Chambersburg, PA 17201
717-267-3738

Del County Pregnancy Center
2508 Edgmont Avenue
Chester, PA 19013
215-872-2229

Pregnancy Center
P.O. Box 401
Clarion, PA 16214
814-226-7007

Airport Area CPC
P.O. Box 1142
Coraopolis, PA 15108
412-262-1220

The CPC
P.O. Box 548
Dallas, PA 18612
717-675-4470

Pregnancy Aid Center
4402 Oeach Street
Erie, PA 16509
814-868-0144

Brephos Pregnancy Center
P.O. Box 576
Gap, PA 17527
717-442-3111

CPC of Adams County
14 S. Washington St.
Gettysburg, PA 17325
717-334-8613

CPC of Kutztown
443 W. Main Street
Kutztown, PA 19530
215-683-8000

Lebanon Pregnancy Center
140 S. 5th St.
Lebanon, PA 17042
717-274-2167

Life House Counseling Center
P.O. Box 1274
Meadville, PA 16335
814-333-6567

Beaver Valley CPC
110 Christy Drive
Monaca, PA 15061
412-728-5550

CPC
P.O. Box 965
New Castle, PA 16103
412-658-6329

Genesis CPC
202 Gay Street
Phoenixville, PA 19460
215-935-1160

Central Pittsburgh CPC
211 N. Whittfield, Suite 480
Pittsburgh, PA 15206
412-661-8430

Monroeville CPC
P.O. Box 633
Pittsburgh, PA 15146
412-373-2775

South Hill CPC
1738 N. Highland Road
Pittsburgh, PA 15241
412-833-2320

CPC of Quakertown
5 South Hellertown Road
Quakertown, PA 18951
215-538-7003

Center Region CPC
114 S. Fraser Street
State College, PA 16801
814-234-7341

CPC of the Poconos
7 South 6th Street
Stroudsburg, PA 18360
717-424-1113

CPC of Wyoming County
P.O. Box 487
Tunkhannock, PA 18657
717-836-4440

North Pittsburgh CPC
P.O. Box 80
Wexford, PA 15090
412-421-3025

Human Life Services
249 E. Philadelphia Street
York, PA 17403
717-854-7615

Rhode Island

South County CPC
43 Mariner Square
Narragansett, RI 02882
401-783-7725

South Carolina

Lowcountry CPC, Suite B 12
2810 Ashley Phosphate Rd.
Charleston, SC 29418
803-553-3528

York County CPC
329 Charlotte Avenue
Rock Hill, SC 29730
803-366-8804

Carolina Pregnancy Center Inc.
P.O. Box 5364
Spartanburg, SC 29304
803-582-4673

South Dakota

Black Hills CPC
520 Kansas City Street #307
Rapid City, SD 57701
605-341-4477

Northern Hills CPC
1231 Poly Drive
Spearfish, SD 57783
605-642-4140

Tennessee

AAA Women's Services
6237 Vance Rd #2
Chattanooga, TN 37421
615-892-0803

CPC Clarksville
1483 Golf Club LAne
Clarksville, TN 37040
615-645-2273

CPC Bradley County
P.O. Box 5183
Cleveland, TN 37311
615-479-6683

CPC of Rhea County
1700 N. Market Street, Apt 28
Dayton, TN 37321
615-365-0019

Cumberland CPC
625 Johnny Cash Parkway
Hendersonville, TN 37075
615-822-1242

Middle Tennessee CPC
106 E. College Ave.
Murfreesboro, TN 37130
615-893-0228

Texas

Amarillo Area CPC
P.O. Box 50342
Amarillo, TX 79159-0342
806-354-2288

Austin CPC
1911 Koenig Lane, Suite A
Austin, TX 78756
512-454-2622

Hill Country Pregnancy Center
P.O. Box 205
Boerne, TX 78006
512-249-9717

Brazos Valley CPC
3620 E. 29th St.
Bryan, TX 77802
409-846-1097

Corpus Christi CPC
P.O. Box 271130
Corpus Christi, TX 78427-113
512-493-9029

Women's Pregnancy Center
10600 Fondren, #102
Houston, TX 77096
713-774-0126

Pregnancy Help Center
P.O. Box 6523
Katy, TX 77491-6523
713-578-0078

Kerrville CPC
944 Barnett Street
Kerrville, TX 78028
512-257-2166

New Braunfels CPC
1281 East Common Street
New Braunfels, TX 78130
512-629-7565

North Dallas CPC
P.O. Box 861614
Plano, TX 75086
214-424-4077

San Antonio Pregnancy Center
2545 Jackson Keller Road
San Antonio, TX 78230
512-377-3610

Women's Pregnancy Center
P.O. Box 304
San Marcos, TX 78667
512-396-3020

Waco CPC
3619 Bosque Blvd.
Waco, TX 76707
817-753-5753

Utah

CPC of Northern Utah
P.O. Box 1673
Ogden, UT 84402
801-393-0511

Preg. Res. Ctr of Salt Lake
805 East 900 South
Salt Lake City, UT 84105
801-363-5433

Virginia

New River Valley CPC
P.O. Box 193
Blacksburg, VA 24060
703-552-3311

Charlottesville CPC
1982 Arlington Blvd #1
Charlottesville, VA 22903
804-979-8888

Southside CPC
116 North Main Street
Farmville, VA 23901
804-392-8483

Peninsula CPC
P.O. Box 7868
Hampton, VA 23666
804-827-0303

Harrisonburg CPC
252 E. Wolfe Street
Harrisonburg, VA 22801
703-434-7528

CPC of Prince William County
P.O. Box 2040
Manassas, VA 22110
703-330-1300

Tri-Cities CPC
P.O. Box 2152
Petersburg, VA 23803
804-861-5433

Richmond Metropolitan CPC
3202 W. Cary St. #200
Richmond, VA 23221
804-353-2320

CPC of Roanoke Valley
2724 B Liberty Road, N.W.
Roanoke, VA 24012
703-362-3007

Page Pregnancy Assistance Ctr
P.O. Box 308
Stanley, VA 22851
703-778-5301

Pregnancy Help Center
21 North Market Street
Staunton, VA 24401
703-885-6261

Pregnant and Single

CPC of Tidewater
258 F No. Witchduck Rd.
Virginia Beach, VA 23462
804-499-4444

ABBA CPC
P.O. Box 3253
Winchester, VA 22601
703-722-4844

Vermont

Tri-State CPC
P.O. Box 1084
Bennington, VT 05201
802-442-2002

Lifeway CPC
21 Belmont Street
Brattleboro, VT 05301
802-254-6734

Burlington Pregnancy Services
323 Pearl Street
Burlington, VT 05401
802-658-2184

Addison County CPC
8 Court Street
Middlebury, VT 05753
802-388-7272

CPC Inc.
P.O. Box 6252
Rutland, VT 05701
802-775-1187

Washington

Heart to Heart Ministries
30620 Pacific Hwy., So., #110
Auburn, WA 98003
206-941-6110

CPC
15935 NE 8th Street, Suite 103
Bellevue, WA 98008
206-644-5232

CPC of Snohomish County
2722 Colby, #403
Everett, WA 98201
206-258-2957

CPC of West Clallam County
P.O. Box 2111
Forks, WA 98331
206-374-5010

CPC of Goldendale
P.O. Box 227
Goldendale, WA 98620
509-773-5345

Lower Valley CPC
P.O. Box 312
Grandview, WA 98930
509-882-1899

Lower Columbia CPC Inc.
P.O. Box 837
Ilwaco, WA 98624
206-642-8717

Crisis Pregnancy Center
5017 196th Street, S.W.
Lynnwood, WA 98036
206-774-7850

CPC of Whidbey Island
P.O. Box 1675
Oak Harbor, WA 98277
206-675-2096

CPC of Thurston County
1416 State Street
Olympia, WA 98506
206-753-0061

CPC of Port Angeles
P.O. Box 39
Port Angeles, WA 98362
206-452-3309

CPC of King County
450 Shattuck Ave., South
Renton, WA 98055
206-235-9660

CPC of Mason County
P.O. Box 1581
Shelton, WA 98584
206-427-9170

CPC of Tacoma Pierce County
1209 6th Avenue
Tacoma, WA 98405
206-383-2988

CPC of Vancouver
214 East 17th Street
Vancouver, WA 98663

Mid-Columbia CPC
P.O. Box 188
White Salmon, WA 98672
509-493-1050

CPC of Yakima
P.O. Box 644
Yakima, WA 98907
509-248-2273

Washington, D.C.

Capitol Hill CPC
323 8th Street NE
Washington, DC 20002
202-546-1018

Wisconsin

APPLE CPC
2600 Stein Blvd.
Eau Claire, WI 54701
715-834-7734

Kenosha CPC
2222 Roosevelt Road
Kenosha, WI 53140
414-658-2555

Ladysmith CPC
115 1/2 2nd N
Ladysmith, WI 54848
715-532-7600

Pregancy Info. Center Inc.
6514 Odana Road, Suite 7
Madison, WI 53719
608-833-1112

Affiliated CPC
2943 N. Oakland Ave.
Milwaukee, WI 53211
414-962-2212

Green County CPC
P.O. Box 13
Monroe, WI 53566
608-325-5051

Wyoming

of Cheyenne
520 E. 18th Street
Cheyenne, WY 82001
307-778-3946

CPC of Jackson Hole
Box 20263
Jackson, WY 83001
307-733-5162

CPC of Albany County
710 Garfield Room 155
Laramie, WY 82070
307-745-3444

CANADA

Alberta

Calgary CPC
#307-1324 11th Ave., S.W.
Calgary, Alberta T3C 0M6
CANADA
403-245-9000

Pregnancy Counseling Centre
Suite 902, 10089 Jasper Avenue
Edmonton, Alberta T5J 1V2
CANADA
403-424-2525

Red Deer CPC
Lower Main 4820 Gaetz Ave.
Red Deer, Alberta T4N 4A4
CANADA
403-343-1611

British Columbia

The Pregnancy Centre
#250 13711 72nd Avenue
Surrey, British Columbia
V3W 2P2
CANADA
604-596-8588

CPC of Vancouver
103-1037 W. Broadway
Vancouver, British Columbia V6H
1E3
CANADA
604-731-1122

143

Manitoba

CPC of Manitoba
809-213 Notre Dame Avenue
Winnipeg, Manitoba R3B 1N3
CANADA
204-947-6699

New Brunswick

The Greater Moncton CPC, Inc.
PO Box 1208, Moncton
Moncton, New Brunswick
E1C 8P9
CANADA
506-857-3033

Nova Scotia

Halifax Metro CPC, $401
5880 Spring Garden Rd.
Halifax, Nova Scotia B3H 1Y1
CANADA
902-422-8539

Ontario

Niagara Life Center
PO Box 779
Beamsville, Ontario L0R 1B0
CANADA
416-563-7021

Belleville Preg. Crisis Ctr.
143 North Front Street
Belleville, Ontario K8P 3B4
CANADA
none yet

Life Centre CPC
141 Kennedy Rd. N
Brampton, Ontario L6V 1X9
CANADA
416-454-2191

London Pregnancy Centre
114p Adelaide St., No., #5
London, Ontario N5Y 2N5
CANADA
519-432-7098

North York CPC
26 Leona Drive
North York, Ontario M2N 4V5
CANADA
416-229-2607

Orillia CPC
6 West Street, North, #307
Orillia, Ontario L3V 6R9
CANADA
705-325-7505

Peterborough CPC
326 A Charlotte Street
Peterborough, Ontario K9J 2V7
CANADA
705-742-4015

Algoma CPC
P.O. Box 1209
Sault Ste. Marie,
Ontario P6A 6N1
CANADA.
705-759-9100

Kitchener-Waterloo Prgncy Ctr
226 King Street, West
Waterloo, Ontario N2J 1R3
CANADA
519-576-5812

Windsor-Essex CPC
1445 Ouellette Avenue, Suite B
Windsor, Ontario N8X 1K1
CANADA
519-973-9888

Quebec

Pregnancy Counseling Centre
1668 de Maisonneuve Quest, #3
Montreal, Quebec H3H 1J7
CANADA
514-935-2122

Saskatchewan

CPC of Saskatchewan
#4-1942 Hamilton Street
Regina, Saskatchewan S4P 2C5
CANADA
306-757-3356